THE TRUE ENLIGHTENERS, PREACHERS AND POLITICIANS

Deepi

Deep Eye Creations

Dedicated to my grandfather, Dr. Dharam Anant Singh Ji, (also known as 'The Sikh Platonist'), the title of whose book gave me the idea for this one.

*"To her fair works did nature link
The human soul that through me ran;
And much it grieved my heart to think
What man has made of man."*

WORDSWORTH

CONTENTS

INTRODUCTION

Exactly 108 years ago, my maternal grandfather, Dr. Dharam Anant Singh Ji (AKA 'The Sikh Platonist') got his first book published in England when he was just about 21 years old. The title of his book, 'Plato and the True Enlightener of Soul' gave me the idea for this book. It set me thinking and I wondered why, despite the prophets or the 'true enlighteners,' we have failed to make progress in getting peace of mind let alone a peaceful world order. I will also like to mention here that I remain ever-grateful to my granddad for sharing his huge personal library with me when I was just 12 years old. It is for these reasons that I dedicate my present book to him.

The sole purpose of this book is to make people think about how we can improve our lives and make the world a better place to live in. It is not a work of scholarship and I hope all who read this book will enjoy it and, at the same time, will be able to use, in some small way, the ideas discussed here to help in making their lives less stressful and the world a more peaceful place. Nothing in this book is intended to hurt anyone's feelings but is to try and make people move towards a less stressful way of life and make a conscious effort towards world peace and happiness.

Though very different from this one, some people may want to read my grandfather's book. It was published in 1912 by Luzac & Co. London and, besides some other sites, is available free at

https://archive.org/details/
PlatoAndTheTrueEnlightenerOfSoulDr.DharmAnantSingh/
page/n25/mode/2up

Deepi, 30 October 2020

CHAPTER 1: THE TRUE ENLIGHTENERS OF SOULS

The King of Brobdingnag's observation on English society in Jonathan Swift's 'Gulliver's Travels' seems true, to a large extent, for the whole human race and many people will agree that we have become "the most pernicious race of little odious vermin that nature ever suffered to crawl upon the surface of the earth." **(Swift)**[1]

The description given above may seem too harsh for our race but if we look at the facts, we will tend to agree. No living being we know of, except the human, treats other species, let alone its own, the way we do. It is, perhaps, for this reason that we alone need so many prophets and preachers. Despite numerous reformers, preachers and prophets, the human race alone goes to war, kills animals for pleasure, profit or medical research, murders others of their own kind with malice in their heart, tortures people and animals, plays havoc with the environment and puts other animals behind bars, in zoos, and enjoys seeing them imprisoned!

Have the gurus and prophets, these 'messengers of God' failed us or have we failed them? What kinds of people were/are these people and can we call them 'the true enlighteners of souls'? Have we become what we are today because of them or despite them? Have the religious beliefs they have given us divided us and caused violence or does the faut lie somewhere else? Not only has religious terrorism raised its ugly head in recent years but even wars have been fought in the name of religion in the past. So, have these people failed completely and become propagators of violence, giving us suggestions that have made us worse than other animals? Before we can think about these questions, we need to consider some other things.

If we peel off their white, black or coloured skin and the somewhat deeper skin of sex of a person and look within, we discover similarities in their blood, bones and cells. We see that each individual is very different yet there is a basic similarity that proves the oneness of the human race despite the individual being externally different. In the same manner, if we peel off the skins of atheistic philosophy, various religious philosophies and spirituality to look both beyond and deep within them, we understand their oneness despite the superficial differences in people's mental understanding and behaviour. Just as in the former case we cannot rationally dislike people despite apparent differences in their colour or sex, in the latter case we cannot detest them because of their beliefs.

Those who have looked deeply and beyond these frivolous beliefs and have experienced the Truth, discovered the reality are the true enlighteners of souls. In this book, to avoid the repetitive use of a long phrase these Experiencers of Reality will also be referred to as prophets, seekers of truth (for they were all seekers before they became experiencers and true enlighteners), spiritualists and so on but the context will make it clear that they are spiritually perfect beings and can be called true enlighteners of souls.

Despite their excellent credentials and contribution to world peace and with no war being fought in the name of atheism, we do not include atheists like Bertrand Russell among the prophets as they have been unable to fill the void created by God in their philosophies. Their logic cannot convince the average person why they should be kind to others and not be selfish except to live in society as a law- abiding citizen to avoid legal hassles which does not convince most people to be kind or less selfish. The agnostic Buddha's belief in the laws of Karma keeps him with the other prophets in this chapter as it explains very well why each individual needs to be compassionate and a better person regardless of whether God exists or not.

There have been many prophets who gave us different religions e.g. the Christ, the Buddha, the Prophet Muhammad, Peace be Upon Him (PBUH), Krishna, Guru Nanak, Kabir and so on. We call them by various names and term them prophets, gurus or even gods, depending on our belief, and say that we follow their teachings. To try and get to the intrinsic nature of religion and to see how far or near most of us are from understanding the religion we call our own, let us discuss a bit of what some of the prophets said, taking a few quotes from them or from the holy books we preach in their names. These have been selected to show the essence of each religion, the philosophy which makes that particular religion what it is or should be if followed correctly. We begin with the **Holy Bible**[2]

"So God created mankind in his own image, in the image of God he created them: male and female he created them." (Genesis1: 27)[2a]. This clearly shows that the Holy Bible treats women and men equally. If they were both created in the image of God, there can be no question that they are equal. The belief that men were created first and women out of Adam's rib in no way contradicts this as even if we believe God fashioned Eve out of Adam's rib, it does not mean that women are inferior as, whatever the source of clay the potter uses, the image that is made depends on the potter. A potter, for example, may make a pot and, before it hardens, take up half the clay that made the pot and create a similar one from it! Would one of the pots be inferior to the other even if their shapes were different?

As for God's true form we may consider this quote from the New Testament: "For God is Spirit, so those who worship him must worship in spirit and in truth." (John 4:24)[2b], If we think how, then, could humans be made in the image of God if God is a spirit, it is clear that the image does not refer to the physical form of God but to the purity of God which becomes clearer from the story of Adam and Eve having the forbidden fruit and trying to be equal to God (and not just the innocent image) in wisdom and knowledge of good and evil. The concept of being 'born again' as given by Jesus in the New Testament is also not physical but refers to the innocence we need to return to. As for Eve being fashioned out of Adam's Rib it implies that men and women are made from the same flesh and bones and are part of the same universal whole created by the power of God. The ribs are the 'holders' of our lungs and even expand and contract when we breathe so are symbolic of life.

We also see the same idea of God being a spirit clearly mentioned by Moses when he talks of idolatry (which is why the image here is physical), he begins with God being without form which is why he says idols should not be made: "You saw no form of any kind the day the Lord spoke to you at Horeb out of the fire. Therefore watch yourselves very carefully, 16 so that you do not become corrupt and make for yourselves an idol, an image of any shape, whether formed like a man or a woman, 17 or like any animal on earth or any bird that flies in the air, 18 or like any creature that moves along the ground or any fish in the waters below. (Deut. 4: 15-19)[2c]. In short, when the scriptures talk of humans being made in God's image, the image referred to is, generally speaking, not physical but when they talk of idols, it is a physical image that is meant."

Now let us talk about Jesus and the images and pictures Christians tend to make of him. As per Wikipedia, Jesus has been described only once in The New Testament and his depiction "in art took several centuries to reach a conventional standardized form for his physical appearance, which has subsequently remained largely stable since that time...The conventional image of a fully bearded Jesus with long hair emerged around AD 300, but did not become established until the 6th century in Eastern Christianity, and much later in the West..." (**'Depiction of Jesus,' Wikipedia.**)[3]

From the above, it can be inferred that Jesus himself did not want people to paint pictures of him or to make his images and statues for he might have thought that people would start worshipping his image. This also seems to be the concern of most other prophets including those who people call gods. From the Buddha to the Christ few, if any, of the prophets' pictures or images seem to have appeared during their lifetime. Having said that, we must also consider the fact that it is very difficult for an ordinary person to talk or even pray to a power they cannot see or imagine for which reason most of us need a picture that we can relate to which is why the pictures of Jesus still vary slightly depending on the culture they are found in.

Does the making of Jesus' images make Christians idol-worshippers as some of the scholars suggest? For a majority of Christians that is not true for they believe in the Holy Trinity which actually keeps them away from idol worship or "putting other gods before" the one and only true God as the three are basically the same. As far as this is concerned, there is absolutely no dichotomy or discrepancy in Christian philosophy as depicted in the Bible and in the lives of most Christians for they do not worship it saying that the image or picture has the power to do something. They pray not to the picture but to God, the power. It is somewhat similar to the Sikhs who always pray to the one and only Almighty, Omnipresent, Omniscient God but may have a picture of their gurus before them or in their minds.

The next quote from the Holy Bible, *is* very relevant even in today's world: "When a foreigner resides among you in your land, do not mistreat them. 34 The foreigner residing among you must be treated as your native-born. Love them as yourself, for you were foreigners in Egypt. I am the LORD your God." (Leviticus 33:34).[2d] It is especially meant for those leaders and people who claim to be Christians but do not want refugees and immigrants in 'their' countries due to one reason or another. It shows clearly that anyone can be a 'foreigner' at some point of time and we need to respect those who have had to migrate from other places. Having said that, we need to clarify that migrants need to respect and believe in the culture, laws and traditions of their new homeland, not try to change them or to go against them while the original inhabitants of that place should incorporate what is better for their society from the 'new' culture.

The Bible also says, "Therefore, you have no excuse, O man, every one of you who judges. For in passing judgment on another you condemn yourself, because you, the judge, practice the very same things." (Romans 2:1).[2e] This goes a step further, when compared to the previous quotes, and tells us not to condemn or judge anyone for we are in no way superior to another human being as we all make the same mistakes which implies that we cannot distinguish between one human and another. Whether man or woman, original inhabitant or immigrant, black, white or colored, we cannot judge who is better and who is worse.

If someone still has any doubts, they need to have a look at this: "There is only one lawgiver and judge, he who is able to save and to destroy. But who are you to judge your neighbour?" (James 4:12)[2f] which makes it even clearer that there is only one judge as God alone has the power over us. We, as people, cannot judge for we are all equal and have no special powers of creating life.

In the final quote from the Bible we take up in this section, "The Sabbath was made for man, not man for the Sabbath." (Mark 2:27).[2g] Jesus states the crux of his spiritual or religious philosophy when he says that the Sabbath is made for the people and not vice versa. It gives us the freedom not yet given by religion. It takes away the guilt of doing something which may ostensibly appear to be going against the laws given by God. He made it clear that it is okay to go against the law when our heart and conscience agree that we are doing the right thing in the circumstances.

Jesus understands the difference between the philosophy based on God's truth and laws given for a period of time, he does not mean to say that all laws are irrelevant or bad but that they are made with the sole intention of improving our lot and if they do not serve that purpose, they are to be overruled as they have lost their relevance, at least for that particular moment, if not period of time as society is in a different phase of development compared to the time when those laws were given. Laws are not meant to destroy or worsen society or individuals but to improve our lot which is why they cannot be relevant forever and under all circumstances.

Here, it is important to digress a bit and discuss an incident from the life of Jesus as it could be misconstrued as an angry outburst by Jesus when he overturned the tables of the money-changers. This 'anger', we need to understand, was not an 'angry anger' for it was not full of malice or hatred but was a 'hurt anger' as he was saddened by the hypocritical behaviour of the people who should have known better. Similar is the case when he curses the fig tree. The fig tree is made to wither for it has lots of leaves but no fruit, like the hypocritical people. It is symbolic of God being hurt by those who say but do not do.

The Christ has shown us how to act in compassion; he, in these incidents, shows us how to 'react' to situations that demand a somewhat violent 'reaction' which is actually not a reaction but a well-thought out response to the hypocrisy he had observed for some time, he demonstrates the way Nature responds when we do something which we should not do, like when we cut trees, we have to face the 'wrath' of nature in the form of a lack of rain. His chasing the money-changers out of the temple is like parents chastising their child out of love, like Mother Nature chastising us so that we can improve our ways. To extend the idea a bit further, we could even say his 'anger' is like an innocent baby's 'anger', there is never any malice in whatever Jesus does and nothing in his life that goes against the philosophy of love and peace.

We can be sure the anger of Jesus was very different from that of most of us for he did not have any malevolence or hatred in him as shown through numerous incidents in the New Testament. He was a person who, knowing fully well he was going to be arrested, healed the servant of the high priest when Peter cut off his ear. It is very unlikely that such a person could be angry in the sense of the word as we normally use it.

We end this section with a beautiful quote from St. Theresa, a saint who lived in our times. Here's what she says exhorting us to take up the responsibility given to us by God, the responsibility of doing good by bringing peace and harmony to the world through love and understanding, as she did herself by serving humanity: "Christ has no body now, but yours. No hands, no feet on earth, but yours. Yours are the eyes through which Christ looks compassion into the world. Yours are the feet with which Christ walks to do good. Yours are the hands with which Christ blesses the world." **(Dillon Maureen, Ed.)**[4]

Prophet Muhammad[5], peace be upon him (PBUH) was also a peaceful person. We will discuss some of his quotes, as per Assad Meah. He said: "The greatest jihad (struggle/striving) is to battle your own soul, to fight the evil within yourself." (Prophet Muhammad, PBUH).[5a] This obviously implies that without battling the evil within us, we cannot fight the evil outside for if we cannot recognise and overcome what is bad within us, we cannot the evil outside. What it also implies is that we have to be perfect to "throw the first stone" at another and once we are pure, like Jesus, we will never throw it. "Feed the hungry and visit a sick person, and free the captive, if he be unjustly confined. Assist any person oppressed whether Muslim or non-Muslim." (Prophet Muhammad, PBUH)[5b] can also go with the previous quotation, in the modern context, as nowadays the leaders of jihad take it to mean the end of other religions and conversion. The reign of terror by some criminals posing as Muslims and misguiding innocent youth surely seems to go against the words and spirit of what Prophet Muhammad (PBUH) said when he talked of assisting people regardless of religion.

"A white has no superiority over a black nor a black has any superiority over white except by piety and good actions." (Prophet Muhammad),[5c] These words of the prophet are again very relevant as 'black' and 'white' refer to the apparent differences in colour but symbolizes the physical differences of all kinds. Where we are born makes us dissimilar in our physical features but these differences are not to be considered to try and put down one or lift another. The only thing to be considered is piety that leads to good actions. By good actions, of course, is meant actions that lead to peace and progress. Anything that goes against society or even a peaceful individual cannot be considered good action or a sign of piety. The word 'piety' does not imply just saying the prayers or talking but piety in the true sense which makes a man or a woman a better human being. It is not a hypocritical or superficial piety but takes us towards universal love and peace between people of all kinds regardless of colour and other differences.

"You do not do evil to those who do evil to you, but you deal with them with forgiveness and kindness." (Prophet Muhammad).[5d] How close this quote is to what Jesus said about turning the other cheek! When the prophet says that we need to deal with those who try to harm us with kindness and forgiveness it is exactly the same as what Jesus says when he wants us to forgive seventy times seven! There is absolutely no difference between this and the Christ's repeated advice to his believers to forgive and not take revenge or have any malice towards anyone. This shows us, beyond doubt, the peaceful intentions in the heart and mind of Prophet Muhammad (PBUH).

"However much the faith of a man increases, his regard for women increases," said Prophet Muhammad;[5e] *and* again,[5f] "The most perfect man in his faith among the believers is the one whose behaviour is most excellent, and the best of you are those who are the best to their wives." These quotes clearly show how some of the people who call themselves Muslims today are very far from what true Islam is and the advice the Prophet Muhammad (PBUH) gives. The prophet Muhammad clearly wants every man to respect not only his wife but also women in general. He would have definitely agreed with Jesus when he saved the woman from being stoned to death. He knew that none of us is pure and so have no right to be judgmental.

Before we talk of any other religion, it would be appropriate to talk about the Baha'i Faith as it is an offshoot of Islam. Like the Sufis, the Bahais do not consider Prophet Muhammad's (PBUH) teachings to be the final revelations of Allah but all that is not relevant here, we will begin with the quotes and what they mean.

The Baha'u'llah[6] says: "Religion without science is superstition. Science without religion is materialism," (Baha'u'llah).[6a] This quote clearly brings out the modern outlook of the Bahai faith, the liberal outlook its propagators had. Directly linking religion to science is perhaps unique to this faith and is a reason for its success among the educated. "Religious fanaticism and hatred are a world-devouring fire, whose violence none can quench." (Baha'u'llah).[6b] The open criticism of fanaticism which makes peace an important component of its philosophy is appreciated by people today and is likely to make this religion more popular in today's world for, though most religions talk of peace the focus is seldom on religious fanaticism and hatred which are aptly described as a "violence that none can quench." We all realize how true this statement is, in these days of terrorism.

Next, we will discuss two quotes of the Baha'u'llah which complement each other: All peoples and nations are of one family, the children of one Father, and should be to one another as brothers and sisters," and, "O ye that dwell on earth! The religion of God is for love and unity; make it not the cause of enmity or dissension." (Baha'u'llah)[6c] Here, the prophet stresses the unity of humankind as all the other enlighteners of souls have done. He says that we all belong to the same family regardless of the country we were born or reside in as we have the same father which obviously does not refer to the physical father but the source, the light from which we all come. He talks of love and unity, not of division. He is very direct when he says that the religion of God cannot bring division or strife for true religion means love and peace. The distinction between 'different' religions disappears as it does in the teachings of the other enlightened souls who sowed the seeds of various religions. Why is it so, why do they all talk of love, equality, oneness and peace? Simply because they had realized God and what they said was based on their own spiritual experiences, not on anything anyone had said without experiencing it.

The last quote we take up for the Bahai faith again reiterates what has been said by other prophets but usually ignored by most people who call themselves religious: "And among the teachings of Bahá'u'lláh is the equality of women and men. The world of humanity has two wings—one is women and the other men. Not until both wings are equally developed can the bird fly..." **(Abdu'l-Bahá)**[7] This final quote in this section talks of the equality of women and men and how society cannot progress unless both of them are developed equally. The comparison to the wings of a bird not only suggests the inter-dependence of men and women for progress but also stresses the perfect equality of the sexes and how necessary it is to take them as equal for the flight of progress.

After the Baha'i faith, let's have a look at some quotations from Swami Vivekananda, one of the most well-known and revered Hindu spiritual leaders of modern times who had not only mastered the Hindu scriptures but was also an enlightened soul. "The best thermometer to the progress of a nation is its treatment of its women. In ancient Greece there was absolutely no difference in the state of man and woman. The idea of perfect equality existed." **(Vivekananda)**[8]. This shows that Vivekananda also believed that women and men are equal. He briefly describes the essence of all religion when he says, "This is the gist of all worship: to be pure and to do well to others." **(Vivekananda)**[9a]. Here, Swami Vivekananda talks of the 'gist of worship' as being pure and doing good to others gives one of the most succinct definition of religion and spirituality possible. He does not talk of doing good to one race, sex or religion but to everyone and he talks, like

Jesus, of being pure, not of being religious.

Let us now take up something which, perhaps, only Swami Vivekananda could have said: "Remember the words of Christ: "Ask and it shall be given you; seek, and ye shall find; knock and it shall be opened unto you." These words are literally true, not figures or fiction. They were the outflow of the heart's blood of one of the greatest sons of God who have ever come to this world of ours; words which came as the fruit of realisation, from a man who had felt and realised God himself; who had spoken with God, lived with God, a hundred times more intensely than you or I see this building.." (Vivekananda)[9b]. This is a beautiful example of complete acceptance and not just tolerance for other religions is exemplified in the third quote where Vivekananda not just quotes the Christ but also praises him – one enlightened soul praising another! What a contrast to today's politician and the 'modern Indian that has emerged in recent years!

"We believe not only in universal toleration, but we accept all religions as true. I am proud to belong to a nation which has sheltered the persecuted and the refugees of all religions and all nations of the earth...I will quote to you, brethren, a few lines from a hymn which I remember to have repeated from my earliest boyhood, which is every day repeated by millions of human beings: "As the different streams having their sources in different paths which men take through different tendencies, various though they appear, crooked or straight, all lead to Thee." **(Vivekananda)**[10]. This quote from this enlightener of the soul does not need much explanation except that the Hindu faith, in its traditional and true form considers different religions just different paths to the same God which is One ('Paramatma').

The concept of 'Paramatma' shows that the Hindus also believe in one God, something like the Holy Trinity being 'one in three' so the Creator, Sustainer and Destroyer would be part of 'Paramatma.' The Idols thus, when initially used by the Hindus, must have been used not as powerful beings but as helping them to pray to God, the Almighty. Dayananda Saraswathi (founder of

Arya Samaj which is part of the Hindu faith), realized this fact when he was just eight years old and saw a rat or mouse climb up the idol of Shiva, then run down and take the food meant for the idol. When Dayananda thought about what he had seen, he realized that an idol that could not protect its own food would be unable to help anyone.

Perhaps the best way to conclude this section on the Hindu religion would be with a quote from an ancient Hindu text which requires no explanation and is relevant for all time:

"May there be peace in the higher regions; may there be peace in the firmament; may there be peace on earth.

May the waters flow peacefully; may the herbs and plants grow peacefully; may all the divine powers bring unto us peace.

The supreme Lord is peace.

May we all be in peace, peace, and only peace; and may that peace come unto each of us.

Shanti (peace) Shanti---Shanti!" **(Panniker)**[11]

The politicians, preachers and people of today need to learn from this ancient quote from the Vedas and from the true enlighteners of souls. Until the time we do so, the global village we claim to live in will remain a physical puddle of putrid mental matter, eons away from both wisdom and spirituality.

Before we move on to discuss Buddhism, let's talk of the Sikh faith. The faith that gave us many new ideas and is known for the perfect equality it maintains between all kinds of people despite religion, sex or other distinctions. The Sikh gurus believed not only in the equality of the sexes but of all humankind. They were so humble that they called themselves gurus, the servants of God and so on, never ever claiming to be God or His sole representative. Guru Gobind Singh Ji, the tenth and last Guru of the Sikhs ended the caste system forever when he instructed his followers to use the last name 'Singh' and to drink the holy *amrit* out of the same vessel. He also made all the castes sit next to one another for *langar*, the free meal for all. All this was unheard of in those times when the lower castes were not allowed to sit with the higher castes let alone eat and drink with them.

The traditions of 'langar' and 'amrit' continue with all who call themselves Sikhs but, unfortunately, there are many among them who have started using their 'caste' as their last name not realizing that they can either be Sikhs or use their 'caste' which clearly owes allegiance to the Hindu faith, especially after Guru Gobind Singh Ji abolished it completely by giving the last name, 'Singh' (meaning, 'lion') to all his followers and abolishing caste within the community.

Now, we must have a look at the philosophy of Sikhism as portrayed in the 'Adi Granth,' the holy book of the Sikhs using some quotes from this great work of spirituality: "He who regards all men as equal is religious." **(Guru Nanak)**[12a]. A short sentence, that says so much! These few words are actually enough to show the greatness of the 'Adi Granth' and to summarize its philosophy. The guru stresses the importance of equality and goes to the extent of saying that a person needs to treat everyone equally to be religious. In other words, the religious must not consider anyone inferior regardless of their sex (men, here, means both men and women), caste and beliefs even if they be atheists. Elsewhere, he says, "I am neither a Hindu nor a Muslim, I am just a human." At the time of Guru Nanak, Sikhism was yet to be born and Hindus and Muslims were the two main religions of India and people of both communities claimed Nanak to be theirs which is why he had to declare that he believed in the oneness of humanity and not in any particular religion. When Guru Nanak talks of treating everyone as equal to be termed religious and of himself being neither Hindu nor Muslim but a mere human being, he has already sown the seeds of the Sikh identity which was later formalized by Guru Gobind Singh to "protect and help the oppressed."

"Realization of Truth is higher than all else. Higher still is truthful living." (Guru Nanak).[12b] When Guru Nanak says that higher than all is the realization of Truth (God), he exhorts us to always look for the truth so that we may actually know God and to do that is the right way of living. This implies that the search for Truth and experiencing it is true religion or spirituality, regardless of the name we give it. It is the true lifestyle that leads us to Reality. This is also a beautiful way of saying how religion and science both look for truth and are complimentary, not opposed to each other. Science primarily wants to know, 'how' while the philosophy of religion tries to answer, 'why.' As always, the words of Guru Nanak and other enlightened souls are loaded with meaning and say much more than they appear to initially convey.

Last of all, in this section, we have the beautiful words of Kabir, another Sufi saint who was revered by Hindus and Muslims alike. Here is what he writes: "First, Allah created the Light; then, by His Creative Power, He made all mortal beings. From the One Light, the entire universe welled up. So who is good, and who is bad? (3) O people, O Siblings of Destiny, do not wander deluded by doubt. The Creation is in the Creator, and the Creator is in the Creation…The clay is the same, but the Fashioner has fashioned it in various ways. There is nothing wrong with the pot of clay - there is nothing wrong with the Potter. (2)The One True Lord abides in all; by His making, everything is made…" **(Kabir)**[13]

The very first line mentions, 'Allah,' the name of God associated with Islam. The inclusion of this verse and other such verses (along with many verses that mention the Hindu names for God) in the 'Adi Granth' is a clear indication that the Sikh gurus were above the distinctions of caste and creed. As Kabir goes on to say, even the distinction of 'good' and 'bad' is illusory as the same life force created us all and the universe. In fact, he goes on to say that the creator and his creation are one which shows that, let alone talk of caste and creed, the true Sikh does not see the difference between 'good' and 'bad', religious or atheist and so on… This very oneness is apparent from the story of Bhai Kanhaya given below.

During one of the battles between the Sikhs and the Mughals, Bhai Kanhaya was serving water to the wounded regardless of whether they were the enemy or his fellow Sikh soldiers.

Some of the Sikhs complained about this to Guru Gobind Singh. The guru called Bhai Kanhaiya and very gently said to him,

"Some of our brave soldiers are saying that you are carrying water for the enemy soldiers as well and they recover only to fight again, do you have anything to say in your defence?"

"Yes, my guru ji. I do that because I see no difference between the Mughal and the Sikh soldiers, for they all have the spirit of God in them. Haven't you taught us that all God's people are the same? Our soldiers are destroying the enemy, I am trying to destroy enmity."

"You have truly understood the message of the gurus," said Guru Gobind Singh, happy at the answer Bhai Kanhaiya had given him. He also gave him some ointment to heal the wounds of soldiers, both Mughal and Sikh alike.

Last but not the least, we consider some teachings of **the Buddha**[14] who said, "If you knew what I know about the power of giving you would not let a single meal pass without sharing it in some way." (The Buddha)[14a]. Here, the enlightened one stresses the importance of sharing and goes to the extent of saying that a person who knows the importance of giving would share every meal "in some way" which could imply sharing with other sentient beings, not just humans. Again, like the other spiritually aware souls, he says, "Believe nothing, no matter where you read it, or who said it, no matter if I have said it, unless it agrees with your own reason and your own common sense." (The Buddha)[14b]. We need to search for Truth, question everyone and everything, not to believe blindly. Once again, a very scientific approach of a spiritual philosopher, a great prophet!

"Teach this triple truth to all: A generous heart, kind speech, and a life of service and compassion are the things which renew humanity." (The Buddha)[14c]. Simple words, easily understood but so difficult to follow! The Buddha talks of serving humanity as a whole, not any particular caste, creed or sex, love and compassion towards all sentient beings remain an important part of Buddhism for the Buddha believed these virtues are essential to the search for truth which is what Buddhism, like other religions, is all about.

We can take up the next two quotes together as they are somewhat related: "Holding onto anger is like drinking poison and expecting the other person to die," and, "What you think, you become. What you feel, you attract. What you imagine, you create." (The Buddha).[14d,e] Both of them are related in the sense that they talk of the mind and the Buddha gives some very practical advice based on his philosophy and experiences. When he talks of anger being like a poison that kills the person who holds on to it, he is giving advice very similar to what modern medical science gives us today. Research has proved that holding on to anger makes us stressed which leads to hypertension, diabetes, heart disease and many more problems for the body and mind. If we think and imagine good things, we become stress free and if we think evil, angry thoughts it leads to stress, disease and an overall aura of negativity through which we are likely to mess up our lives. Much before modern psychology was born, the Buddha knew of the power of the mind and that of positive thinking!

After carefully analysing what has been said above, we cannot but help agree with the following: "All religions, in their pure form, will tell you God is Love. And power, fear, division, judgment, oppression, hatred and self-righteousness are the opposite of Love. So, going to war, for example, in the name of religion, is a complete contradiction. No pure religious leader would ever support this." **(The Truth AD Infinitum)**[15].

As is apparent from what has been written above, no religion has taught violence yet we have seen the Crusades, the massacre of Muslims in Myanmar and of Tamilians in Sri Lanka by people claiming to be Buddhists, the persecution of the Parsees and Bahais in Islamic Iran, the killing of Sikhs (1984) and Muslims by those who said they were Hindus, the killing and persecution of Kashmiri Hindus, the days of Sikh terrorism in the Indian state of Punjab and elsewhere, Islamic terror, the list goes on…

Why does this violence occur despite all religious books

giving the message of peace and oneness? Why does this happen when we are well aware that violence benefits no one and History is replete with examples of the most powerful people not being able to enjoy the fruits of wealth and power for very long? How did the preachers, politicians and people start talking about division on the basis of religion, race and nation? And, when all the true enlighteners of souls left the judgment to God or to karma, when and why did we become judgmental? Why do the people follow others instead of drawing their own rational conclusions even today when most of them can read and write and have access to the scriptures and what the true enlighteners of souls said as much as the preachers do? What has caused the problem or problems? We need to think about these issues…

Notes & References:

1. Swift, Jonathan. 'Brobdingnag: History and Government'.' Wikipedia. Retrieved on 6 Oct. 2020 from

https://en.wikipedia.org/wiki/Brobdingnag#:~:text=The %20King%20of%20Brobdingnag%20finds,the%20surface %20of%20the%20earth%22

In Jonathan Swift's novel, Gulliver's Travels, when Gulliver describes to the King of Brobdingnag, the English people's actions and behaviour, the king compares the description to his own people and makes this comment

2. Holy Bible. These quotations from the **Holy Bible**[2a-g] are very popular and available on multiple sites on the internet which is why the websites have not been given and only the places where they are to be found in the Bible are mentioned. **Quotation No. 3** is, unfortunately, an unavoidable intrusion as it is **followed by some more quotes from the Bible.**

3. 'Depiction of Jesus.' Wikipedia. Retrieved on 20 Sept. 2020 from

https://en.wikipedia.org/wiki/Depiction_of_Jesus

4. Teresa, Saint. Dillon, Maureen. (Ed.) (n.d.) '14 Of The Most Powerful Peace Quotes From St. Teresa of Ayla.' The Mystical Humanity of Christ Publishing. Retrieved on 12 Aug. 2020 from

https://www.coraevans.com/blog/article/14-Of-The-Most-Powerful-Peace-Quotes-From-St-Teresa-Of-Avila

5. Muhammad, Prophet.[5a-f] Meah, Asad (Ed.) (n.d.) '35 Prophet Muhammad Inspirations Quotes.' Awaken the Greatness Within. Retrieved on 07 Aug. 20202 from

https://www.awakenthegreatnesswithin.com/35-inspirational-prophet-muhammad-%EF%B7%BA-quotes/

6. Baha'u'llah[6a-c]. (n.d.) 'Baha'u'llah Quotes.' Goodreads. Retrieved on 07 Aug. 2020 from

https://www.goodreads.com/author/quotes/2926126.Bah_u_ll_h#:~:text=Bah%C3%A1'u'll%C3%A1h%20quotes%20Showing,who%20may%20cross%20your%20path.%E2%80%9D&text=%E2%80%9CBe%20generous%20in%20prosperity%2C%20and,a%20bright%20and%20friendly%20face.

7. 'Abdu'l-Bahá. (n.d.) 'The Promulgation of Universal Peace.' Selections from the Writings of 'Abdu'l-Bahá, (sec. 227, p. 302.) [7]. Retrieved on 07 Aug. 2020 from

https://bahaipedia.org/Gender_equality#:~:text=%22And%20among%20the%20teachings%20of,remain%20weak%2C

%20flight%20is%20impossible.

8. Vivekananda, Swami. 'Swami Vivekananda on Women and Womanhood' (08 Mar. 2016). Desh-Videsh. Retrieved on 16 Oct. 2020 from

https://www.deshvidesh.com/swami-vivekananda-on-women-and-womanhood/

9. Vivekananda, Swami[9a,b]. (n.d.) 'Swami Vivekananda's Quotes that will Inspire You to the Fullest.' Quote Nos. 2 & 6 in the source. (26 Jan. 2018). NewsGram. Retrieved on 07 Aug.20202 from

https://www.newsgram.com/swami-vivekananda-quotes/

10. Vivekananda, Swami. (11 Sept.1893). 'Swami Vivekananda and His 1893 Speech.' Art institute, Chicago. Retrieved on 09 Aug. 2020 from

https://www.artic.edu/swami-vivekananda-and-his-1893-speech

11. Panniker, Raimundo (transl.) 'The Vedas.' (n.d.) World Healing Prayers Retrieved on 12 Aug. 2020 from

http://www.worldhealingprayers.com/5.html

12. Nanak, Guru.[12a,b] (n.d.) 'Guru Nanak Quotes.' Goodreads. Retrieved on 07 Aug. 2020 from

https://www.goodreads.com/author/quotes/333495.Guru_Nanak

13. Kabir, Sant. (n.d.) Prabhatee (trans.) 'Spirit Voyage.' Sri Guru Granth Sahib. Retrieved on 08 Aug.2020 from

https://www.spiritvoyage.com/mantra/aval-allah-noor-upaaya/man-000443.aspx

14. Buddha.[14a-e] (n.d.) '108 Buddha Quotes on Meditation, Spirituality and Happiness.' Posted by Hannan Hutyra in Keepinspiring.me. Retrieved on 07 Aug, 2020 from

https://www.keepinspiring.me/buddha-quotes/

15. The Truth AD Infinitum, 'The Truth AD Infinitum Quotes.' Goodreads. (n.d.) Retrieved on 07 Sept. 2020 from

https://www.goodreads.com/quotes/tag/the-truth-ad-infinitum

CHAPTER 2: WE BELIEVE…

A preacher, a lawyer, and a doctor go out in the forest, hunting. They all spot a deer grazing. They all shoot at it at the same time but they only find one bullet hole. They cannot ascertain who shot the deer, each wanting to claim the trophy of a kill so they decide to call their friend, who is a Wild Life Expert, to come and examine the deer. They tell him where they all stood, that they shot it at the same time, and that it dropped immediately. He looks at it for quite some time, thinks deeply and finally says:

"I know who shot the deer"

"Who?" They all ask eagerly.

"It was the preacher."

The preacher shouts for joy, while the other two are furious.

"How can you tell that just from looking at the bullet hole?" They ask angrily

"Well it's really very easy." He says calmly. "If you look at the bullet hole, you can see that it goes inside one ear, and comes out the other"

This may be a good joke but is not very accurate for people do listen to their preachers, especially in the **'developing' and 'underdeveloped' countries.**[1] Most people, including political leaders and teachers are influenced by them. Many of them try to follow what their preacher tells them and sometimes what they hear them say in childhood leaves a lifelong impression on them, becomes a part of their psyche. This includes politicians, dictators and monarchs. We often hear people from all walks of life say:

"I believe in religion..."

"I believe in God..."

"I think..."

"I dream of becoming..."

"He said, I feel..."

All of us are creatures not only of belief but also of dreams and emotions. Preachers, teachers and leaders are no exceptions. Our beliefs usually depend on what we hear or read and these beliefs influence our 'new' thoughts, ideas, emotions, dreams and what we say. Since they are all inter-related, this order may vary but that is not the issue here as our main concern, at the moment, are beliefs.

Believing in one thing or another should not cause problems but many of us, including our preachers, take our beliefs as the Gospel Truth, the Only Truth and are willing to argue, fight or even die for them not realizing that beliefs may or may not be true as they depend on our perceptions which, in turn, are based on how our personal experiences have affected and shaped us as individuals. These personal experiences not only include our upbringing, education, social norms prevalent at the time, what we are made to think the scriptures say and the influence of people close to us but also many other things including any traumatic experiences we might have had. Our preachers' and politicians' beliefs are also shaped by these factors.

It is for this reason that, if we talk about religion or spirituality, what we believe is usually based on the interpretation of a religious text which is meant for another person (generally, the preacher or parent) for we have not read even our own scriptures independently and rationally. Similar is the case with our political or other beliefs as we are invariably influenced by others instead of approaching everything in a rational, thoughtful and analytical manner analysing the influence of our own experiences and meditating on what we have heard or read.

When we talk of preachers, we cannot deny the fact that some of them are not only excellent human beings but are also very open to others' beliefs. They not only try to pass on their interpretation of the scriptures but are open to others' interpretations too. They study a lot, sincerely try to find what in their scriptures is relevant for their congregation at the current time to create positive feelings, give them courage and play their role in bringing peace and harmony to the world. One such person gave a sermon on forgiveness.

He talked about Christ's message of forgiving "seventy times seven." After the sermon, someone in the congregation asked him about what he thought of the common idea of "forgive and forget." He thought a while, then said that, in his opinion, forgiveness was important but we should not forget. To prove his point, he quoted the story of Joseph (from the Old Testament) in which Joseph forgives his brothers but does not forget how they tried to harm him. The reason he gave for his belief was that if we forget and do not learn our lesson, we are likely to be fooled again by those who want to harm us which is why the Christ also said we need to be "as innocent as the dove and as wise/cunning as the serpent."

However, what some preachers preach could be rather controversial or, in a few cases, even malevolent. Regardless of the religion they belong to, they do misguide the people. Those who do that could be politically motivated or somewhat selfish as they, like you and me, are part of the society we all live in but most of them actually believe in what they say and, we can say with conviction, that not many, if any, of them are bad people who intend evil towards society as a whole.

How can we say that most preachers and religious leaders, who usually start their careers as preachers, do not intend evil? For the simple reason that no preacher takes up this profession to do evil. It is extremely unlikely that, before going to bed, any preacher would consciously plan the evil s/he intends doing the following morning or get up in the morning and say, "Let me see what evil I can do today!" They too, like many politicians they influence, actually believe that they know the truth and take it as their moral duty to guide the masses into their interpretation which they truly believe is good for each individual and for society as a whole.

Just as no political or other idea is true for all time, religious interpretations differ from time to time. The scriptures speak to us for our own selves, to improve ourselves and those like us. They are not meant to be interpreted by someone for everyone. Religious texts are not for us to argue and kill for an interpretation of what is written in them and communicated to us by our preachers. If they were meant for arguments and killing, they would cease to be religious and become instruments of terror as some people have made them.

The scriptures main, if not the only purpose, is to make us better human beings so that we can build a society that strives to move towards perfection which is the other name for peace, harmony and blissful happiness that leads to God. This can perhaps be made clearer through an ancient Indian story (found in one of the *Upanishads*) which goes something like this...

Long, long ago the *manusas* (humans), the *devas* (benevolent, divine beings) and the *asuras* (evil, supernatural beings) sought advice from the Creator, Prajapati.

The *devas* were the first to ask Prajapati to advise them who simply replied, "*Da!*" The *devas* thought about it for a while after which he asked them, "Do you understand?"

"Yes Lord," they replied, "*Da* stands for *damyata* or self-restraint."

The Creator smiled and told them they were right and must control themselves as they were very powerful.

Next, the *manusas* or humans asked Prajapati to advise them and the Creator repeated the same letter of the Sanskrit alphabet, "*Da,*" and then asked, "Have you understood?"

They replied immediately in the affirmative and said, "Yes, Lord you mean *datta*- to give," for the humans were very intelligent and had many good qualities but were selfish.

"Yes," replied Prajapati looking pleased with the answer.

Last of all, the *asuras* who were very strong but cruel and evil asked the Creator for advice to live life by. They, too, got the same answer, "*Da.*"

They pondered over the advice given to them for long, then Prajapati asked them, "Have you understood what I mean?"

"Yes, yes Lord," answered the *asuras*, "By 'da' you meant *dayadhyam* or compassion."

Prajapati was happy with the answer and told them it was good that they had understood. He was not judgmental, nor did he provide any interpretation. He accepted all the answers which they gave as he knew wisdom is of use only at the level it is required and understood.

This is also true of the scriptures and we all need to understand this. We cannot gain anything if we listen and believe the interpretation relevant for the past or of a person who is at a different level for the *deva*, the *asura* and the human are all within every individual in different proportions. If we repeatedly read the scriptures sincerely, with faith and in a humble manner to improve ourselves as human beings and not to judge others, we will get what we need.

We need to be aware of our own problems and take from the scriptures whatever is required for our spirit, the way the *devas*, the humans and the *asuras* did. The role of the preacher, therefore, is to motivate and encourage people to read the scriptures or to listen to them with an open mind and get from them what is relevant for them. Preachers, like Prajapati, need to be open to various interpretations and willing to support whoever listens to them in getting what they need as individuals. Like teachers, they have to ensure that each person gets what their mind and soul needs. The sermon, of course, has to be general but it should be delivered. in such a way that it is clear to the listeners that it may or may not be meant for them and they are free to ask and to give their opinions on it as it is not the Only Truth. Exactly what some good preachers, like the one who gave the sermon on forgiveness mentioned above, do.

However, most times, that does not happen. Most religious preachers, of all faiths, somehow seem to convince the people that their religion is superior to other religions, some castes and/or races are superior or inferior, men are superior to women and so on…Why do they do this? And how do they succeed in this present world when almost everyone can read and write? As mentioned before, they all are not insincere, evil women and men who preach others to be like them. Neither are people with so much exposure to the internet and seemingly quite intelligent and well-read evil. So, does the problem lie elsewhere?

This happens because our existence, as perceived by most of us, depends on our beliefs and we, including our preachers and teachers, generally take another's interpretation of their truth as our own truth or even The Truth for which we are willing to argue, fight, kill or even die. We are willing to kill, we are willing to die but do not try to find out the truth relevant to us by going directly to the scriptures with the intention of improving ourselves, unwilling to behold "the beam in our eye." Faith, an essential element of religion, spirituality and life itself, becomes a problem creator instead of being a problem solver, as it was originally intended to be.

What has happened is this: our misplaced faith has made us complacent; it has made us forget that we cannot afford to be satisfied with someone else's truth or even with our own and fall into the abyss of judgmental ignorance. We have to search for and experience The Truth instead of taking the easy way out of making others' beliefs our own. The scriptures and the true *gurus* can be guides or catalysts but the experience has to be our own. No one can make us 'see' or experience God, the Holy Ghost or The Truth that is hidden behind the words of the scriptures or the prophets and awaits our realization through the awareness of our own shortcomings and taking remedial measures to overcome them. This is what our preachers need to guide us into so we can improve ourselves and shape our beliefs based on more love and compassion, as the prophets wanted us to.

Whenever the godmen and women, the false prophets and others who are misguided themselves, grow powerful enough to misguide a majority of us, a true prophet, a seeker and propagator of truth is born to lead and guide those who are willing to listen into the heaven of eternal peace, truth and both internal and external harmony by questioning their false beliefs and awakening their conscience. We may or may not believe in the Second Coming but history is witness to the fact that, whenever violence and falsehood predominate, a prophet or true guru arrives to try and enlighten the minds and souls of the common people who are confused but have the desire to seek and to know. But, these enlighteners of souls have all succeeded only to a very small extent as our education and our preachers have not made most of us ready for them and they, the prophets, do not scatter their "pearls before the swine" we have made ourselves into.

Not only do many preachers portray their interpretation as being the only one but most of them, instead of talking about the philosophy, focus on the laws and rituals actually believing in and effectively conveying to the people they are for all time while the fact is that laws of religion, like all other laws, need to change because civilizations develop and cultures change as do people and their character.

Every prophet is/was aware that culture is dynamic and ever-evolving, growing richer with the influence of other cultures. If it were to block outer influences, it would stagnate and become irrelevant. The only thing new about **such a culture**[2] would be the kinds of new germs of violence and ignorance it grows which would be of interest only to the Mephistophelian among us.

Just as cultures grow and develop into better and more beautiful cultures, religions grow richer and better when new prophets like Jesus and the Sufis arrive to reform them. Whenever this happens or when a culture grows or changes in any way, there is a need to change the laws. With positive development or deterioration in the overall character or morals of a community or any other changes, the laws too, need to change. And then, there are things like industrialization e.g. when there was no internet, there was no cyber-crime and so no laws for the same were required.

It is very necessary for us to read what the prophets say for ourselves, not just listen to our preachers' explanations, to get to the meaning which will improve us as human beings making us more loving, compassionate and spiritually alive. If we do not become better and more compassionate, there is surely something wrong with our understanding and we need to discuss it with our preacher or read our scriptures again. The test of truth is its ability to make us better and more compassionate. That is what true Islam is. That is what true Christianity is. That is what true Hinduism or Buddhism or any other religion is.

Our preachers need to tell us and we have to understand that, though philosophy is more important than the laws and rituals of religion, it can be interpreted differently by different people. Any religious thought, whether it be law and ritual or philosophy which goes against the basic idea of love and compassion given by the prophets, would be rejected outright by any rational or truly religious person as such a person is always spiritual.

Anything which goes against humanity, preaches violence of any kind or creates division cannot be the work of any true prophet or God and it either means that the interpretation of the scripture is incorrect or it is meant for another time or kind of person. This is not understood by most people, some of who follow these incorrect interpretations and create divisions on the basis of race, caste, creed, region, sex and numerous other things in the human race itself, let alone talk of generating hatred and cruelty towards other species of animals. May the people of all faiths and beliefs experience and express this truth so that they can form the right beliefs to make the world a better place and not be influenced into violence and war by the rich and powerful or by their own erroneous beliefs based on their parents' or preacher's interpretations.

Sometimes, the preachers using their personal understanding of the religious texts/scriptures as the only true interpretation and influencing people, including politicians and all kinds of leaders may be sincerely trying to serve the people not realizing that it actually harms society instead of helping it. Most of the people who hear the sermons, like those who give them, take them as the only truth and unthinkingly swallow the medicine meant for another. It is like a healthy person taking the chemotherapy meant for a cancer patient or a heart patient taking the medicine for malaria. The damage it can do is immense. It is we, the people, who have to understand for the preacher who is involved will find it difficult to do so.

Many people in positions of power who claim to be religious read their religious texts through the minds of their preachers that usually focus on the laws and the rituals in the book. They rarely try to follow its philosophy which is more difficult to comprehend but is actually what the spiritually advanced true enlighteners of souls want us to focus on for it is this philosophy alone that is for a long period of time, if not forever. As mentioned earlier, the laws and rituals are definitely a reform for the time they are written but have little relevance as time elapses and society progresses.

As the laws were given for a particular time so there might be an element of violence in them e.g. "an eye for an eye, a tooth for a tooth" could have been a major reform for the time when people probably took lives for an eye or a tooth. As society of the time was not developed enough to understand and practice the modern systems of crime and punishment (as we see them in countries like Norway, Sweden, Bhutan and Switzerland), it was necessary to have some kind of violence in return for violence. As mentioned earlier, Jesus Christ hinted at the necessity of change in laws when he said, "the Sabbath was made for man and not man for the Sabbath," apparently contradicting the laws the traditional people of his time believed to be 'true' for all time. The Christ, like all other spiritual giants, understood that the laws are not true or false but are meant to serve society (of the time in which they were given) in the best possible way.

Religion cannot teach violence or division as the enlighteners of souls were spiritually advanced souls and spirituality invariably brings people closer to one another and promotes love. In fact, like Bhai Kanhaya whose example was given earlier in the book, a true spiritualist sees the same spirit of God in everyone. If we understand this fact, we will never base our beliefs on violence, hatred or negativity even if someone tries to misguide us, using their beliefs based on the misinterpretation of our scriptures. We will then believe in the basic goodness of humanity, like Jesus did, and will forgive everyone without being judgmental but taking care that we are aware of and do not fall prey to the views of those misguided into malevolent beliefs. That is what the true and sincere preacher would teach us, that is what our prophets teach us and that is what we need to learn from our scriptures.

Notes & References

1. In the 'developed' countries not many people go to churches, mosques, temples or other places of worship so is not directly relevant to such countries, their problem is actually the opposite and will be discussed later. The situation is very different in the countries that are not so rich, financially and are called 'developing' or 'underdeveloped.'

2. This is relevant to culture alone and not to religious books as they cannot change with time though their interpretations should and do change.

CHAPTER 3: THESE PEOPLE IN POWER!

We have been talking mainly of beliefs and preachers in the previous chapter; now, we will talk a little of politicians and other people in power. Both preachers and politicians often quote the 'true enlighteners of souls,' the spiritual giants who sowed the seeds of true religion. And true religion, of course, is an expression of the spiritual experiences of realized souls who have known the reality of love and compassion beyond the comprehension of ordinary mortals who are engrossed in their daily chores, unthinkingly wasting their precious lives in lust, anger, greed, attachment and pride of their intelligence, unaware of the fact that the wisest of humans know that they know little. As Socrates put it, "I am wiser than this man, for neither of us appears to know anything great and good; but he fancies he knows something although he knows nothing; whereas I, as I do not know anything, so I do not fancy I do." **(Socrates)**[1]

There is no doubt that some leaders of religion and politicians form a nexus, for money and power, and influence the general public in a negative manner (including but not limited to the hatred of other religious beliefs), something similar is well-expressed in the following quote:

"Look at the tyranny of party-- at what is called party allegiance, party loyalty-- a snare invented by designing men for selfish purposes-- and which turns voters into chattels, slaves, rabbits; and all the while, their masters, and they themselves are shouting rubbish about liberty, independence, freedom of opinion, freedom of speech, honestly unconscious of the fantastic contradiction; and forgetting or ignoring that their fathers and the churches shouted the same blasphemies a generation earlier when they were closing their doors against the hunted slave, beating his handful of humane defenders with Bible-texts and billies, and pocketing the insults and licking the shoes of his Southern master." **(Mark Twain)**[2]

The above quote from Mark Twain not only talks of the hypocrisy which has been a problem at least since the time of Jesus but also hints at the nexus, perhaps based on their beliefs steeped in ignorant selfishness, between the leaders of religion and politicians. Many of whom we call the *intellectual class* also tend to agree, especially in the 'developing' and 'underdeveloped' countries, that the problems of the common person are due to the 'unholy nexus' that exists between politicians and leaders of religion who misguide preachers and the public through them while in most of the 'developed' countries it is the politicians who are controlled by the rich and powerful businesspersons and/or multinationals. In fact, even in the 'developing countries' the role of the rich is prominent both in religion and politics for they 'donate' and buy whoever they can.

Many of our leaders/politicians, like us, are selfish, greedy and corrupt. They come from within us and so are similar to us, most of them no better and not much worse than the general public though they get more opportunities for corruption.

Like the common man or woman, some political leaders think they are wise but are not even intelligent so, like the proverbial Shadwell and the rest of us, they "rarely deviate into sense." If they were more sensible, they would have learnt from history not to repeat the mistakes made by leaders of religious terrorism like Osama Bin Laden and the likes of Hitler and Col. Gaddafi who had to suffer a lot and die dishonourable deaths, they would surely be intelligent enough to know they cannot fool "all the people, all the time." However, we can see the leaders of today making the same mistakes as were made repeatedly in the past by other leaders. This does not mean that they are evil but implies that they are either misguided or unaware of the reality as perceived by the general public and genuinely feel they are doing the right thing for the people and looking after their own selfish needs and ambitions at the same time. Of course, there are some among them who do actually think they can fool everyone forever but they are in a minority.

One thing is for sure that whether evil or not, these leaders, along with the rich and powerful, are responsible for the deterioration of the environment, for the overall mess that we are in and for the scourge of war which is, perhaps, the evillest of crimes which any animal species has ever witnessed on earth.

"The object of war is not to die for your country but to make the other bastard die for his." **(Patton)**[3]. These words of General Patton may be good to motivate soldiers to fight a war but do not show the reality of war. It does not tell them that those who try "to make the other bastard die for his country" have an equal chance of being killed for theirs. It does not say anything on the family that will remain after the soldier is killed, it does not tell the soldiers that may be maimed for life or even have to live in a vegetative state. It is ironic how, read another way and taken out of context, this quote can mean that people in power do not die for their country but make the poor soldiers die for their country!

Patriotism forgets humanity and, when used to attack another country instead of defending one's own, is the antithesis of human values. The worst part is that war is not declared by the soldier but by those who have no intention of seeing the battlefield. This is brought out very well in Thomas Hardy's, 'The Man He Killed' in which a soldier describes how he joined the army just because he needed a job and, in a battle, killed a soldier on the opposite side as he was supposed to be his enemy but might have joined the army as, like the narrator, did not have another job. He killed the "enemy" despite the fact that neither of them knew each other and, if they had met each other in an inn, they would probably have had a drink together or even helped each other in some small way. In other words, the decision to make war was not of the soldiers but of the rich and the politically powerful who use everything from religion to the concept of patriotism for their own selfish ends.

A highly decorated, US Marine Corps Major General (Retd.), Smedley Butler also had similar views on the reasons for war and wrote, "War is a Racket: It always has been. It is possibly the oldest, easily the most profitable, surely the most vicious. It is the only one international in scope. It is the only one in which the profits are reckoned in dollars and the losses in lives. A racket is best described, I believe, as something that is not what it seems to the majority of the people. Only a small 'inside' group knows what it is about. It is conducted for the benefit of the very few, at the expense of the very many. Out of war a few people make huge fortunes." **(Butler)**[4]

According to the same source (Wikipedia), Butler suggests that, to end war, it has to be made unprofitable. This can be done by 'conscripting' those who make profits out of war (e.g. industrialists and capitalists, executives of armament and steel factories, ship-builders and airplane builders, bankers and speculators) before conscripting young people. He says that acts of war should be decided by those who fight it and are at risk of dying at the front lines. He also suggests that war should be only for self-defence and "the Army restricted to the territorial limits of the country, ensuring that war, if fought, can never be one of aggression."

Besides the people mentioned by Butler, it would be a good idea to conscript the sons and daughters of politicians and of the top army brass who are involved in the purchase of weapons. Looking at the present scenario, it would, perhaps, be essential to also conscript those in the media who support war, and if they are too old, at least one of their blood relatives.

Politicians, like the media and many of us, are aware of the fact that we tend to believe a polished lie more than we do the truth. Knowing this fact fully well, we still believe the media and the politician when they lie to us as we lack the capacity to think well enough to counter a lie a politician has skilfully delivered. To deal with the lies of the media and politicians, we need the philosophical honesty and ruthless bluntness of a Diogenes which has always been a scarce commodity found among the rarest of rare individuals. Let alone think deeply and honestly, we are not even in the habit of thinking originally nor do we have the time to do so in the present world of computers, entertainment and politics.

Tahsin a well-travelled and observant young man at the time, a former colleague of the author of this book, once remarked that all governments of the world conspire to keep their people busy in different ways so the public do not question what the people in power are doing. When the author asked how that happens, a conversation followed that went something like this:

"In the capitalist countries, the governments have made entertainment so cheap, people just don't care what the government does, whenever they have time, they either go out to watch a movie, go for a swim, to the beach or just watch some television at home while in the communist world, Vodka is so cheap, they get drunk and forget all their problems after a tiring day at work."

"What about the developing and under-developed countries?"

"Oh, people hardly have time to think in those countries, they're too busy trying to earn their bread and butter and to save for the rainy day as there's hardly any social security."

"And what about the Middle East?"

"Here, they don't really get any time from their prayers."

It is difficult to say how true this is but what he said is really worth thinking about. Whether it is a conspiracy or simply lack of time or it is a problem with the education or the influence of media, the fact remains that we rarely question what our governments do till it is too late and the damage has been done. In most countries of the world, regressive systems that are not conducive to thought prevail and most of us are not even aware of it! The result is an overall sense of frustration among the people.

Abusive language can be heard when people talk about politicians or others in power the world over bur few have the capacity or the inclination to think why they are leading an unhappy life full of greed, stress and an unhealthy, competitive ambition. Some people may not agree with such views and say that the systems that are in place in their country are the best possible and their leaders are doing a good job but the fact remains that the majority are of the opinion that those in power could do more to make them lead a better and happier life. They know something is wrong and, if those who are at the helm of affairs work in a different way, things for the common women and men can be much better than they presently are. However, a vast majority of them are unable to figure out why they are suffering and what can be done to improve the situation.

It is a fact that kings, queens, presidents and others who are or have been in power in most countries, have not been able to keep their citizens happy – at least not most of them. They have used ways to gain and remain in power that have ranged from petty to cruel, they have used money and muscle, threats and kind words so that they can get or retain power.

In many countries where absolute poverty exists, money is used to win elections. Some political parties in such countries distribute blankets or some other gifts just before the elections. They even give bottles of liquor and/or a small amount of cash to people who are poor to purchase their votes.

Heads of state are generally aware of the fact that, unless the people are happy, they cannot stay in power indefinitely. They know that even kings, queens and powerful dictators have had to face revolutions and revolts. They have been unable to retain power for their whole lifetimes without public support so there is little chance for the survival of democratically elected leaders to return to power in the following elections. Why is it, then, that they do not look after the welfare of their people and keep them happy? Why do they have this short-sighted approach?

Most kings and queens had and numerous present-day politicians have enough money to last generations, more power than any other person in their respective countries but they all continue on the path of death and destruction to become more and more powerful and grab as much money as possible (a greater portion of which they or their progeny will never be able to use.) They say they are working for the people but the people are not happy! Why do they continue? It simply does not make sense.

The Buddha, it is said was a prince before he started his search for truth. Here's a part of his story: "Do not let your son see an old person, a sick person and a dead person," the wise men are supposed to have told the King, "if you don't want him to give up the royal path and be a seeker of truth." As soon as he saw the 'forbidden three,' it is said, that Prince Siddhartha, the future Buddha gave up his kingdom to tread 'the invisible path' to enlightenment. On the other hand, most people in absolute or democratic power continue to order the killing of people both in war and even in routine politics. They not only see the old, the sick and dead like we all do but actually order murders and go to war which leads to loss of life on a large scale. It just does not make any sense....

Now, let's discuss a hypothetical conversation that could actually take place in any office in many countries of the world...

"Sir, the road has been made," the engineer told his officer, the district collector.

"How long will it last without any potholes?" the officer wanted to know.

"Well sir, we didn't use sufficient or standard material so it's likely to be in pretty bad shape after the rains."

"Well, it is a problem but we can handle that. What about the bridge you completed last year? I hope that'll last a while."

"That'll last another four years or more, sir."

"Oh, that's okay, the next government will be in power and we'll both be transferred by that time anyway and blame it on someone else. Have you got your cut?"

"Yes, sir," said the engineer with a smile.

"So, you are satisfied…I still have to send the minister her share."

The above situation has been created as an example for this book but this kind of a conversation is quite common and, especially in the developing countries, people can easily relate to it. The ministers, officers, engineers, contractors and others responsible do not seem to realize that they too use these roads. There is no doubt that they are what we term selfish, corrupt criminals but their behaviour seems to be based on their ignorance.

Yes, they are transferred but wherever they go the situation is likely to be the same as others like them have got the work done there. And, of course, they think they will never retire! They do not seem to realize that they are part of the public and use the same facilities. The underhand money stops coming when they retire and they end up using the same bad infrastructure their whole life! Like Alexander, who at the time of his death realized he could not carry his riches with him, those of them who do realize their mistake, realize it too late! They realize they have been ignorant and foolish but can do nothing to rectify their mistakes as they no longer have the power to do so. In frustrated anger, they blame one thing or another and eventually die in forlorn sadness.

Her husband was talking to Anita of such issues when something like the following conversation actually occurred:

"Something very similar to this happened in Kanpur, only it was more tragic than just travelling on roads with potholes," said Anita.

"I hope it's a true story, not a made-up one," her husband asked.

"Well, I was very young so can't be a hundred percent sure but that's what my mom told me and she said it had come out in the papers," Anita answered, looking a bit offended.

"I do trust my mom-in-law and her daughter," he smiled...

"So, would you like to hear what happened?"

"Yes, of course."

"It was all over Kanpur and even my friends were talking about it at the time..."

"Well, what was it about?"

"An engineer, I forget his name, was in charge of a bridge constructed somewhere in or around Kanpur and, soon after it was built, it collapsed, killing hundreds of people who were on it at the time."

"Well, that's not very uncommon in India, is it?"

"The engineer's son was also one of those who died!" Anita ended dramatically.

This is reportedly a true story and there are many other such stories which appear in newspapers all over the world. Yet, we all continue sowing what we don't want to reap!

It is strange that no one looks for the reason in a positive way. We all become negative, saying "this was long overdue, such people deserve what they get" or something like, "But these people are never going to improve whatever the lessons God tries to teach them." We, the people, actually join such leaders if we can to get our pounds of flesh. Instead, we need to find out the reasons for such behaviour and then to look for solutions; yet we are more interested in finding faults and indulging in negativity or getting some benefit from the corrupt, thus becoming part of the evil, hypocritical system and dishonestly portraying ourselves as honest and/or pious people.

Another thing that is used to gain or retain power in a democracy is division on the basis of race, sex or any other kind of tactic to divide the people. But then, is it not strange that people are divided so easily when, in today's world, they fully understand that their blood groups are not based on race, religion, caste, colour or sex. How do they believe the politicians and others who fool them to gain power or to remain in it? What makes us so gullible? Is it the big, bad politician to blame? Or, does the problem lie somewhere else?

The reason, whether it be selfishness or greed or whatever of our leaders, it is usually not the 'evil nature of a person' as some of us think. A religious person may say "it's the work of the devil," an atheist may blame it on the evil in human nature but the question remains, why??? Are some of us born bad? Is it genetic? The answer is not easy but we need it in order to find a solution to the problem. However, before we do that, it is essential for us to look at a few great leaders, both who are considered 'evil' and those most of us think are 'good.'

Two of the people we will consider – Hitler and Genghis Khan - were (and still are) considered evil, or at least cruel, by most of us while we tend to praise and even idolize Abraham Lincoln and Gandhi for what they did. Let us, first of all, consider Adolf Hitler who, generally speaking, is looked down upon even by Germans today.

Most of us do not know much about Adolf Hitler but consider him evil as what he did was cruel and evil but the evidence suggests that he personally was convinced that he was a very intelligent man who wanted to make his country great, create a 'superior race' to improve the world or even make it a perfect place. He definitely thought he was doing the right thing in killing innocent people to create enough 'space' for the 'superior race' in Germany and to remove the 'weak' or 'inferior races' from his country and then, perhaps, from the face of the earth and so had no qualms about getting innocent people put in ovens and gas chambers.

Had Germany won the war, he would have been made a hero by the Nazis. But would that have been morally right? Many or perhaps most of the Chinese in mainland China think that the subjugation of Tibet was the right thing to do. Despite all the avoidable killings that occurred in Iraq and Afghanistan, the American public were made to believe that American intervention in those countries was right. Similar was the case of Vietnam when many Americans called Muhammad Ali a coward for not fighting a war which he felt had nothing to do with him or his country.

Thousands of innocent people were killed during the cold war period for different reasons (e.g. oil) in many countries where the major world powers of the time wanted titular heads of state who would toe their respective lines. The comparisons, though inappropriate in scale when compared to Hitler's evil deeds, are very similar in intention in the sense that they were all based on the false belief that it would be good for the people of their respective countries. No one seemed to realize that violence is not good for humanity and what does not benefit the human race as a whole cannot be good for anyone and eventually harms everyone.

Governments, in the modern world, have often resorted to violence when the heads of state have had strong beliefs like those of Hitler and others like him. These people in power have actually believed they were doing the right thing as they tend to convince themselves and others of their righteousness and think they are doing good by killing people not realizing that no war or killings can be good or right except in self-defence or in an attempt to prevent brutality as was the case when Lincoln got slavery abolished. We need to understand that the evil in the world can be due to actions that may stem from false notions of 'doing good' or improving our countries or making the world a 'better place' by supressing others with the use of malevolent violence.

Similarly, as per figures given in Wikipedia, even though Genghis Khan was responsible for the death of around 40 million people (most historians agree on that), he cannot be termed evil for he "practised meritocracy and encouraged religious tolerance in the Mongol Empire, unifying the nomadic tribes of Northeast Asia. Present-day Mongolians regard him as the founding father of Mongolia." (**'Genghis Khan', Wikipedia**)[5]

Despite the Civil War, it cannot be denied that what Abraham Lincoln did to abolish slavery was righteous and done for a noble cause. Similarly, Gandhi's achievement of getting freedom from the powerful British through peaceful means was not only noble but also showed the power of peace over violence. Times changed, corruption grew in the world, governments became more powerful with lethal weapons but the power of goodness and peace were proved again by Nelson Mandela when he got freedom for his country through these very means. So, what made these three and other leaders like them great human beings despite their human failings? What made Hitler a cruel and dreadful evildoer in the eyes of people? It was the difference in the kinds of dreams they had and/or the paths they adopt to achieve them.

While Gandhi and Mandela dreamt of bringing freedom and harmonious equality among the people of their respective countries, while Bertrand Russell dreamt of making the world a place of peace and harmony, Hitler thought of war to compete with and dominate others, of 'ethnic cleansing' and of bringing more countries under German control in a violent fashion. They all dreamt big but the difference in their respective visions made them belong to two very distinct classes. And the difference in their dreams and their levels of ignorant selfishness and negativity was due not only to their personal experiences but also because of their understanding based on the education they got or gained from their experience. We will talk more about education or the lack of it, despite the best of schooling for jobs, in another chapter which will answer the questions posed in this one.

As mentioned earlier, the *asura* (symbol of evil) is in all of us but it leads to evil action only if it dominates the *manusa* (human) and the *deva* (godly) to make our beliefs and consequently our dreams unreasonably violent, narrow, selfish and/or malicious. The dreams of Mandela, Gandhi and Lincoln were based on their positive and constructive ideas of equality while Hitler's dreams were based on his ideas of negative and competitive 'superiority' that led to needless violence and most despicable and evil of acts known to Nature and humanity – War! War, a symbol of ignorance and an uneducated, irrational, short-sighted mind! Had he won the war and the Nazis made Hitler a hero, the truth would have still come out eventually for it is virtually impossible to suppress all the people for eternity.

Whether it is a powerful government/leader or a powerful religious organization that involves the people in violence, a Mandela is always born to oppose it, a Galileo to question it, a Christ to guide the people out of it...

Notes & References

1. Socrates. Lodhi, Anam (Ed.) (02 June 2018) Socrates on Wisdom. Retrieved on 22 Sept. 2020 from

https://medium.com/indian-thoughts/the-only-true-wisdom-is-in-knowing-you-know-nothing-5789c8994cc6

2. Twain, Mark. (n.d.) 'Autobiography of Mark Twain Quotes.' Goodreads. Retrieved on 08 Oct. 2020 from

https://www.goodreads.com/work/quotes/13039075-autobiography-of-mark-twain-the-complete-and-authoritative-edition-vol

3. Patton, George S, (n.d.) 'George S. Patton Quotable Quotes.' Goodreads. Retrieved on 08 Oct. 2020 from

https://www.goodreads.com/quotes/9169410-the-object-of-war-is-not-to-die-for-your

4. Butler, Smedley. 'War is a Racket.' Wikipedia. Retrieved on 14 Sept. 2020 from

https://en.wikipedia.org/wiki/War_Is_a_Racket

5. 'Genghis Khan.' Wikipedia. Retrieved on 16 Aug. 2020 from

https://en.wikipedia.org/wiki/Genghis_Khan

CHAPTER 4:
PROBLEMS AND
THEIR CAUSES

If we look at what Christ, the Messiah and the other true enlighteners of souls said, we discover the difference between they thought and how we have been trained to think about religion by parents, preachers, teachers and politicians. Socrates, the Buddha, Christ, Prophet Muhammad, the Sikh Gurus, the Baha'u'llah, Swami Dayananda Saraswati and others were major reformers because they were against hypocrisy and did not fear to talk about the Truth they had experienced even if it appeared to contradict established religious laws and beliefs.

The true enlighteners were messengers of peace and most of them tried to look for the good and peaceful in existing scriptures and tried to interpret them in a way that was conducive to love, peace and a stress-free, harmonious life for a maximum number of people. The best example of this is, perhaps, the reconciliation of the Old and New Testaments by Jesus.

It is an 'ironic pity' that, for the reasons discussed before, laws of religion, meant as reforms for the peoples of the time they were given in, sometimes become major hurdles in the progress of society. One of the examples that can be taken to prove this point is the opposition to a law pertaining to euthanasia based on the belief that it is against the laws of religion. It is amazing how Christians killed their wounded horses (in battle) and still put their sick dogs "to sleep" to relieve them from their pain but will not show mercy to their own species, their near and dear ones, when they are suffering from a painful terminal illness like cancer and express their willingness to die.

An example of how the absence of a religious law is misused is that of smoking and doing drugs. Smoking and drug abuse were virtually unknown when most major religions of the present world were born so there are no rules or laws mentioned on those. Alcohol abuse is, for example, forbidden in Islam but nothing is said about drug abuse because it simply did not exist at the time. Because of the same reason, most religions are silent on smoking with the result that, despite both drug abuse and smoking being more harmful than alcohol, their abuse depends on the country we live in and the preachers and politicians of that country but had drugs or smoking been common in the days of Christ and Prophet Muhammad, their use would have surely been prohibited as would have been other things that did not exist at the time but do now. A good example would be that of pornography or 'obscenity' on television and films. What is pornography and what is obscenity depends on the level of maturity of a person and the culture s/he lives in. What is art to one may be obscene to another so, had it been directly mentioned as a law in the scriptures, it would have been another recipe for violence at different stages in history.

Anyone who has been involved in any kind of literary or philosophical research is aware that the researchers look for examples to support their theses from various sources and successfully find them. Unlike the prophets, we have been trained to look for the differences rather than the similarities in the different religions and instead of trying to reform them like the prophets did, we tend to think of them as permanent, universal commandments and focus on the laws and rituals – the easiest and the most obvious to consider rather than the unifying but somewhat abstract philosophies of religion, much more difficult to comprehend especially if they are written in a literary style. This is one of the major issues that is the cause behind religious strife today, as it was in various times in history. Similarly, we focus on the colour, nationality, political and religious beliefs rather than the underlying humanity and the life force behind and within sentient beings.

As mentioned in an earlier chapter, some politicians and other leaders use race and religion to play on the emotions of people in order to gain their selfish ends. More often than not, religion has and is still being used by leaders to gain power, whether it be for their selfish ends or in the 'hitlerian' belief that they are helping their country and its people. How do they manage to gain power? It is because the centre, the mind, *does not* hold and all kinds of dogmas ranging from the political Left and Right to that of various religious dogmas gain popularity among the people and this is used by politicians to fool the gullible public for they do not think or are incapable of doing so.

"As Mencken put it, Indeed, it may be said with some confidence that the average man never really thinks from end to end of his life. There are moments when his cogitations are relatively more respectable than usual, but even at their climaxes they never reach anything properly describable as the level of serious thought. The mental activity of such people is only a mouthing of clichés..." **(Mencken)**[1]

This is a major issue, the root of many other problems: Most of us do not think on our own. Whether it is the religious belief, the influence of our friends and family, political belief or. a lack of training to be better human beings, the fact remains that we are creatures of belief and our beliefs are generally not based on rational thought relevant to the present reality of our situation nor is it geared to make a violence-free, better environment for humans and other sentient beings. When they are related to other sentient beings, our beliefs are usually even more steeped in ignorance than those in which humans are involved. Here is an example to prove this point:

Lobsters, in many 'developed' countries are put in boiling water to kill them for food in the belief that they feel no pain despite the fact that Sir J.C. Bose and others after him proved that even plants feel 'pain.' In fact, Aldous Huxley, when he visited Bose's laboratory in Calcutta said something to the effect that, if vegetarians happened to witness his experiments, they would stop eating vegetables! Pleasure, pain, sadness, death, happiness are all part of nature and we sometimes cannot avoid giving pain or even death to other sentient beings but doing so in the erroneous belief that they are not feeling pain is simply proof of our ignorance that stems from our inability or disinclination to think or rationalize for ourselves. That is the mother of most problems that society faces today and has faced for some time.

Another problem is our apathetic hypocrisy. An example of this is the murder of dogs that are not taken by anyone for two weeks in most parts of the 'developed' world, the ill-treatment of 'mother cow' in India, the 'culling' of kangaroos in Australia (can be sterilized) and the killing of 'pests' like rabbits and other beautiful creatures Mother Nature has provided the earth with. Instead of thinking of other alternatives like sterilization or building animal shelters instead of wasting money on bombs, the first thought that enters our minds is to kill them as they are 'lower forms' of life. This is happening despite numerous people who claim to be dog lovers, animal lovers and animal rights activists many of them not even writing against such murder. This, too, is due to our lack of thinking as we do not realize that needless violence that starts with other species makes us so used to it that we do not bat an eyelid when it happens to our own human race.

We will not say much about the problem of belief and how religious laws are taken as eternal and interpretations of religious philosophy taken as the gospel truth as these have already been discussed and we will briefly talk about it again. So, let us move on to the next problem which is selfishness (the cause of which is generally fear e.g. the fear of losing a job or money or not having enough money.)

This selfishness due to fear was prevalent even in ancient

times as can be discerned from numerous examples. The kings made their incompetent sons their heirs to the throne ignoring more competent people as they feared the end of their dynasty. The caste system in India was, initially, not rigid and a son or daughter did not necessarily have to be the same caste as the parents. There are various explanations given by people on why it became rigid which led to the ill-treatment of the 'lower' castes but the most plausible one seems to be that those who once graduated to the higher castes did not want their incompetent children to again fall into the lower castes. Consequently, in their selfishness, they ensured their progeny were protected forever, not realizing or not caring about the immense harm it would do to society and, in the process, to their own future generations like the engineer who did not realize his son could be killed when the substandard bridge he got made collapsed, killing his son. Such people do not realize that what they think is benefitting their children eventually harms them. Once again, the problem behind this selfishness (which is a kind of fear – the fear that their children will not do well in life) was and remains the inability to take thoughts to their logical conclusion.

As in the past, in present day society too, if a person feels his or her profession is good, they want their children to follow suit though teenagers generally have the freedom not to do so in most countries today. In some 'developing' countries though, the situation is quite different and parents literally force their children to become doctors, engineers, lawyers and politicians especially if they, themselves are in those professions. This happens even if their son or daughter is interested in something completely different like art or philosophy as their parents think they know what is good or otherwise for their children. This belief, too, as can be easily seen is based on the fear that their children will suffer if they do not take up the profession they are being forced into. How incompetent and unhappy such a person would be in the profession s/he is forced into and the damage that will be done to society and to herself/himself as a result is anybody's guess.

When we talk of selfishness, an old story comes to mind. Some greedy fish in the pond ate more than they needed to. They did not listen to the wise fish who told them to "eat to live, not live to eat." Soon, the plants were finished and they started eating the other smaller creatures in the pond. Eventually, there were none left and the bigger fish started eating the smaller ones till only two were left. The bigger of the two ate the comparatively smaller one and then died of hunger. Similarly, for centuries, we have concerned ourselves only with our selfish pleasures and luxuries, destroying 'others' thinking of differences based on family, race, country or species. As the human race, we have not cared about the environment around us as we have thought only of ourselves, our competitive 'progress' and 'development.' How long can this be sustained is anybody's guess.

It would be a good idea to talk again about violence even if it means being accused of too much repetition. It is good to talk about this repeatedly as the subject is too important to be forgotten and needs to be re-iterated frequently in this book.

When we talk of the true enlighteners of souls being apostles of peace, we must not forget that some spiritual giants, despite their firm belief in non-violence, had to fight to defend people against the atrocities perpetrated (many times in the name of religion) by those in power. As Guru Gobind Singh said in his *Zafarnama*, "When all other means fail, it is fair to unsheathe the sword." To defend themselves against brigands and predators, it was the Buddhist monks who developed the martial arts but then, as the author's Karate teacher told him years ago, "If you can run, run - don't fight! The martial arts are to defend yourself when your life is in danger and there is no escape." This violence is like the violence in Mother Nature though they are not the same in scale or in substance.

The malicious and selfish violence of an ordinary human differs greatly from the hate-free earthquakes, Tsunamis, disease and 'natural death' that exist in Nature. This is also the difference between the violence of a spiritually advanced guru like Guru Gobind Singh and Nature on the one hand and that of most ordinary people, political leaders and terrorists on the other.

Nature's violence usually occurs when, knowingly or unknowingly, we break its rules and exploit it, it is an attempt to recover and to set things right, a balancing act. Nature turns violent to save the life-force or to create life like the death of a caterpillar leads to the birth of a butterfly, the death of a seed gives a beautiful plant and so on. Similarly, the violence of a spiritual person is to protect life or to restore some kind of balance. It never stems from any negativity or hatred.

So, what is it that causes destructive violence with no constructive, restorative purpose or balancing act involved? Is it some kind of inherent evil in man? In most cases, the answer would be a big, 'NO!' Why? For the simple reason that, due to many factors, the people who are the architects of this senseless destruction, especially on a large scale, actually believe they are right. As already discussed in some detail, even Hitler seemed to genuinely believe that what he was doing was the right thing and it would do his country good without realizing that when humanity suffers, everyone suffers eventually.

Just as Hitler and Genghis Khan cannot be termed evil for their evil violence as they believed in their dreams which they did not consider bad, we cannot say that the evil of terrorism today is due to the evil inherent in some people. Like Hitler talked of a superior race and obviously believed in it, most terrorists today either think they and their people have been exploited or believe that 'immoral' people have to be converted or killed for an ideal world to be created. Although we cannot term such people evil, their actions are surely evil because there is malice in their hearts for their 'enemy' whether the 'enmity' is in the name of religion, race, politics or for some other reason. In contrast to the 'true enlighteners of souls,' they have no capacity to think in a positive, rational manner. And adopt 'negative rationality' to prove their beliefs to themselves and others who are of the mob mentality.

As discussed in an earlier chapter, it is not the belief that is the problem but the fanatical rigidity with which some people adhere to those beliefs. When such people come to power, they wreak havoc on the world and eventually harm themselves and the people they consider their own. There are at least two reasons for this. The first is some sort of insecurity which is usually due to an unhappy childhood or some traumatic experience at a young age. The second is relying on others (could be preachers, teachers, the media), for the creation of our beliefs which most of us feel are correct even though only a few of us are fanatical enough to fight or die for them. This is more of a problem when the 'other' relies on yet another who has quoted out of context or read only the quote! Once again, it all boils down to the problem of irrational fear and the inability to think in the right manner as anyone who thinks positively would read the context, especially if the quote seems negative.

Most of us, including our political leaders, are in the habit of quoting out of context which spreads misinformation among the general public who do not read the complete text and rely on quoting the truncated quote. To clarify this point, let us take an excerpt related to the **'Macaulay Minute of 1835'** from this author's book, 'You, Me and Little I," which, though fiction, has many facts woven in its pages. Excerpt:

"Thank you, I'm Shilpa Sharma from Delhi. My question is for Randall. You said Christians have given the world schools and universities, but in India they were opened to serve British interests. Macauley, for example, said-"

"Sorry to interrupt," said Randall, "but I think I know what you've got on your mind, Shilpa. I hope I've got your name correct..."

"Yes, you have..."

"Well, Shilpa, Macaulay has been quoted out of context."

"How do you mean, out of context?"

"I'll clarify what I mean," Randall paused to shuffle some papers he carried with him and resumed, "I need to read from his famous minutes which have been widely condemned in India but not properly read or understood. I quote, 'It is impossible for us, with our limited means, to attempt to educate the body of the people. We must at present do our best to form a class who may be interpreters between us and the millions whom we govern: a class of persons, Indian in blood and colour but English in taste, in opinions, in morals, and in intellect. To that class we may leave it to refine the vernacular dialects of the country, to enrich those dialects with terms of science borrowed from the Western nomenclature and to render them by degrees fit vehicles for conveying knowledge to the great mass of the population.' He also says that western education is likely to awaken ambition that will make the Indians seek freedom and that it will be a proud moment for the British.' Unquote. I hope your question is answered."

"Yes, thank you very much. It's amazing how we consider people bad, based on government propaganda."

(Deepi)[3]

Shilpa, in the above conversation represents millions of people in India who, without reading the actual text of what Macaulay said, trusted what they heard being propagated by the political parties in power at various times in Indian history to instil a sense of patriotism in the people by promoting negativity among them. They portrayed Macaulay, for example, as a villain who wanted to kill Indian thought by making them clerks with "English ideas" forever serving the British. This was initially used by some Indian states to remove the English language from their schools a few years after India got Independence from the British in 1947. Later, many of these states realized the advantages of teaching an international language at a young age and re-introduced it, the private schools took the initiative and made Indian children proficient in the language thus giving them an edge over China and Japan as these countries realized the advantages of teaching English at a much later date along with many European countries.

People have felt the need to have an international language for a long time and, in 1887, Esperanto was presented with the hope that it would serve as a language to communicate with people the world over. Even though this artificial language is much easier to learn than languages naturally developed over a period of time, peoples of the world did not accept it as a language of communication because the world was not so well-connected at the time.

However, due to increased travel, international trade and commerce English emerged as an international language of communication. Initially, countries like China, Japan, France and Germany did not accept it but now, realizing its importance, it is being taught at some level or another in those countries. Some Indian politicians regardless of their political affiliations, on the other hand, taking 'research' and the views of 'experts' into consideration stir up the 'patriotic spirit' and start an anti-Macaulay campaign from time to time to 'reform' education. The realization that experts can be wrong and that research findings change with time, researcher and sponsor has yet to dawn on them so both present realities and historical facts are ignored. This is because they can discern only the colours they want to see in the picture they are looking at from an angle that appears to suit them.

It would be a good idea to relate to language, what we said of culture earlier. We all need to realize that language, like religion belongs to the world not to individuals or countries. Languages, religions and cultures must be influenced by other languages, religions and cultures to grow and prosper. If that does not happen, a language degenerates and may even die, a religion becomes obsolete by moving away from the spirit of what the person who started it said. A cocooned culture, of course, is the worst affected as both language and religion form part of it. Such cultures, stagnated by narrowmindedness breed bacteria of the mind that stink. The stench grows till the rest of the world shuns such cultures shaped by ignorant negativity, and trampled on by those who are incapable or unwilling to think with an open mind, thus destroying from within, what they are ostensibly trying to save.

People usually do not accept these facts because it is difficult for most of them to see the whole spectrum and much easier to see a part which they presume is the whole, they think what they have seen is the whole truth and nothing else could be greater, better or more true than their perception based on their little experience and even less thought. They are so similar to the frog in the well...

There was a frog who lived in a well near the sea. He was a happy frog, in his little well and never wanted anything in his life which he could not get there in his little world. One day, another frog fell into the well.

"Where do you live?" The frog in the well wanted to know.

"I live in the sea."

"Is it as big as my well?"

The frog from the sea was amused but understood that his friend who lived in the well had never ventured out so, very gently, tried to explain.

"No, no it's much bigger," said the frog from the sea, "In fact, there's no comparison."

"Is it this big?" The frog who inhabited the well jumped from one end of the well to the other.

"No, no. the sea is so big you cannot even imagine it unless you see it."

"You are a liar; I don't believe you."

Most of us are like the frog in the well and believe our religion, our culture, our thoughts are the greatest and the best. We refuse to think with an open mind.

We need to open up, we need to view the whole spectrum, not the colours we want to see. As Gandhi put it, "I do not want my house to be walled in on all sides and my windows to be stuffed. I want the culture of all lands to be blown about my house as freely as possible. But I refuse to be blown off my feet by any." **(M. K. Gandhi)**[4]

When we talk of not being blown off our feet, it does not mean that we do not accept other cultures and enrich our own through them but that we have to consciously reject anything in another culture that is not as good as we already have in our own. We definitely need to accept that part of another culture, religion or thought which improves us, makes us better human beings and makes us socially progressive and is good for our society e.g. Raja Ram Mohan Roy turned against the tradition of Sati (burning of widows) and Gandhi went against the system and culture that created the 'low-caste' untouchables in India.

We need to remember that culture is not something static, it is dynamic and changes with time with or without the influence of other cultures. It is said, there was a time in the Victorian era when people in England covered the legs of their sofas and chairs simply because they were called 'legs' so could not be left without clothes while India had Khajuraho, symbolising sexual freedom centuries before that. We also need to remember that religion, language, culture and all else that has enabled or led to human development and social progress are not the birth right or property of any individual, country or region but belong to the whole world, to humankind if not to all sentient beings. But, unfortunately, that understanding is not happening, that remains the problem.

The politicians, ignoring the whole, consider just a small part as the complete whole and the people follow their lead; preachers focus on the laws and rituals of religion either ignoring the philosophy or giving their own rigid interpretation of it and saying it is the only correct one. The result is that the tings God would not object to, the prophets and gurus would not judge are judged and objected to by most people because they are not into the philosophy of religion but are convinced by the powerful speeches of those they trust.

As the story goes, the bus conductor would not allow the bus to move until the lady with the dog left the bus or went to the empty upper deck. She refused to leave or go up, saying it was very cold and the little dog was friendly. All the passengers were getting late so supported the lady and wanted the bus to continue with its journey.

The conductor was firm and quoted the rule that said no dogs were allowed on the bus and was adamant, saying the bus would not move till the lady followed the rule. He was being liberal, he said, and had already compromised more than enough by allowing her to sit on the empty upper deck which the lady had refused as she felt it was too cold and the dog was small and harmless. At last the lady agreed to go up and the triumphant conductor, just before the last stop, when no other passenger except the narrator was left on the bus, asked him if he had done the right thing. The narrator of the story replied that he had kept the rule but broken its spirit as rules are made for the comfort of the people, not to harass them.

The narrator's comment in the story above, as we can see, is very similar to what the Christ said when he talked of the Sabbath being made for man and not vice versa! Whenever a preacher, politician or anyone else who we respect says something which could lead to violence in any form or seems to go against the spirit of humanity or social justice, the people must thoroughly debate it, exploring all sides with an open mind. This is especially true of the laws and rituals we find in the religion we profess allegiance to but is also true, to a large extent, for any idea given by anyone. Are most of us capable of doing it? The answer is in the negative and that is a problem!

We need to talk a bit more about the media as we discuss the problems that lead to violence and ill-will among the people and also the lack of thought. There is no doubt that in modern times, the media has played a great and positive role by letting people know what is happening around the world but it has also had its drawbacks. An example will make it clearer: The fourteenth century Italian poet, **Dante**[5], in his *Inferno* (Hell), Canto XXVIII places the Prophet Muhammad (PBUH) and his son-in-law Ali in the eighth circle of hell meant for "sowers of discord." Dante was not killed in a terror attack while the **'Charlie Hebdo'**[6] office was attacked for a cartoon they published. The attack occurred due to the publicity it attracted in the media, including the internet. Had today's media existed in Dante's time, he would have very likely been killed.

The media should actually make people think in a positive manner but, somehow, despite the debates on TV and the internet, despite social media it has had the opposite effect on many people. Most people unthinkingly believe what they see and read to be true. They do not seem to realize that the media is a double-edged sword. It gives different viewpoints and sometimes people are more influenced by the negative than they are with the positive. At times, it also is a tool in the hands of those in power who use it to propagate their ideology or belief or to simply keep the people busy in various controversies so they do not think of their own exploitation.

Politicians and religious leaders also sometimes use the media to dupe people into a patriotic or religious fervour with the bogey that one or the other out of them is in danger as there is likelihood of war or of terror from another religious community. They generally do this at the time of elections or when the economy is doing badly so that people's minds are diverted and they think of the 'danger' instead of the real issue/s that affect them.

The media, even when it is research based and educative, can sometimes have the potential to cause problems. The BBC documentary, **'Jesus was a Buddhist Monk'**[7] is a good example of this. The documentary tries to prove that Jesus did not die on the cross and he went to India where he was influenced by Buddhism. It does concede, however, that he and his disciples probably did not lie and believed he had died as he was unconscious. If they did not lie and it had no negative effect on his teachings, why on earth do we want to research this and 'prove' he did not die on the cross knowing fully well that it can be a controversial issue with a big potential for problems between the believers and those who do not believe in Christianity? If the purpose was to prove that Christian and Buddhist philosophies are similar, that could have been done in better ways e.g. taking extracts from what Jesus said and comparing it with what the Buddha said. Does it really matter if he went to India or not? Can we ever really be sure of it?

Whether Jesus was crucified or not and even whether he rose from the dead or not is a debate for those who do not have faith in his teachings, who do not firmly believe in his love and compassion so has the potential for strife and violence as such people may not believe in his concept of peace and forgiveness. If we think a little more about this, it should not really matter to the people who believe in him, whether or not what he taught was similar to what the Buddha taught.

The negative influence of some preachers, politicians and the media has led to a few of us insisting on the laws and rituals of religion as the way shown by God. Those of us, thus influenced, believe everyone else is 'immoral' and needs to be made moral and 'religious' not realizing that we are being judgmental and going against our own religion in doing so. The extremists among us turn to terror, coercion and a whole lot of other anti-social ways to 'convert' others to our belief. This has actually made many detest the 'religious' and consequently religion itself. They are either professed atheists or have a vague idea of 'some power; that may be working somewhere which we cannot understand so it's better to live a life of luxury and material comfort without caring for anything else. In other words, they have given up religion but have had nothing to replace it which could sometimes lead to drug addiction and many times to depression. This has become a major issue today especially as in schools, in secular countries, there is no moral education worth its name.

As Blaise Pascal put it, "What else does this craving, and this helplessness, proclaim but that there was once in man a true happiness, of which all that now remains is the empty print and trace? This he tries in vain to fill with everything around him, seeking in things that are not there the help he cannot find in those that are, though none can help, since this infinite abyss can be filled only with an infinite and immutable object; in other words, by God himself." **(Blaise Pascal)**[8]

This was written a few centuries ago but is even more relevant today than it might have been then when it was written. In today's world, religion no longer has the prominence it had in most people's lives at the time. However, the few who are religious, believe their preachers and politicians who often focus on the laws of religion or the preacher's personal interpretation of its philosophy many a time taken out of context.

As repeatedly **emphasized,**[9] the philosophies of religion are similar, if not the same, but quite difficult to understand e.g. the parables and humans have always looked for easy solutions. God would not object, the prophets and gurus were not judgmental, people are! They do not generally delve deep into the philosophy of religion but remain on the surface, under the influence of some preachers and/or politicians focussing on religious laws and narrow interpretations.

A story that some of us may have heard and which explains, in a better way, how we become judgmental and go against what God wants is that of a young ascetic who, once upon a time, lived alone in a forest, He never ate anything until the time he could feed at least one person every day before he had his first meal. One day, it so happened that no one passed by his hut till noon. Very hungry, he fervently prayed to God to send someone. At last an old man appeared, walking slowly down the path in front of his hut. Happily, he went to meet the stranger and asked him to have some food in his "humble hut." The old stranger readily agreed and the ascetic invited him in where he placed some food for him on a banana leaf.

"Let's pray before we eat," said the ascetic.

"I don't pray, I'm an atheist!"

"What, you're an atheist!?!"

"Yes, I am."

"Get out! I don't feed those who don't believe in God."

The ascetic threw him out in anger and, as soon as he calmed down, went back to his prayers. He was famished but continued to pray for a person he could feed so he could eat without breaking his self-imposed rule. Finally, he heard a voice:

"But I sent you a man, why didn't you feed him?"

"He didn't believe in You! How could I feed him?"

"How old do you think the man might have been?"

"He must have been 65 or 70…" answered the young ascetic.

"I fed him for 70 years and you couldn't give him one meal? Do you deserve to eat?"

The ascetic felt sorry for being judgmental and prayed sincerely for another chance. Late in the evening, he was happy to apologize and feed the same old man who, on his return journey, was taking the same route. He not only fed him before he ate himself but even offered him shelter for the night and a meal the next morning before he left for home.

Hardly any preacher, regardless of his or her religious beliefs, would tell such a story for it shows God's love for humanity and not alone for the religious. This story also illustrates part of the problem that creates fear in the minds of people and fear, in its different forms, leads to all kinds of problems. The story above shows, how, scared of displeasing God, the ascetic was willing to keep a fellow human hungry even at the cost of remaining hungry himself.

Looking at the problems listed above, we may conclude that the basic problem is that of accepting the thoughts of others who are not competent enough to get to the truth because most of us are incapable or unwilling to think rationally and with an open mind. Not only are we afraid to think on our own but, even if we do, we are scared we may be wrong or may look foolish so we fail to express ourselves in fear.

If we analyze the idea of courage in war, it is also based on different kinds of fear. Why, for example, does the soldier kill the 'enemy' despite having no personal enmity with the soldier on the other side? It could be simply the fear of being killed, if we do not kill. Or, it could mean the fear of losing honor and prestige, the fear of being called 'unpatriotic' while in an ideal human society there would be no scope for patriotism for equality and fearlessness would prevail and no one would be exploiting another regardless of where they are born or live.

Selfishness is the cause of many kinds of anti-social activities e.g. when we think only of ourselves, we try to earn more and more money to satisfy only our craving for luxury or 'security.' We think first of our own body, then the family, friends and so on without caring for others. When we see our lives are in danger or we are likely to remain hungry, we even resort to criminal activities to ensure no harm comes to us or our families. Once again, the cause behind this selfishness is fear - fear of hunger, of death and sometimes that of 'insult' that may lead to a lack of compassion for others.

Some fears are instinctive, like the fear of losing one's life or the life of a dear one. Even this fear was eliminated in the prophets. Abraham was willing to sacrifice his son's life, the Sikh gurus and many of their disciples had also overcome all kinds of fear including that of death. These people were very religious, very spiritual but today's average 'religious' man or woman is full of fears – not only the animalistic fear of death but the fears of failure, of dishonor, of old age, of sickness (even of the doctor and the tests they conduct), of suffering in hell or on earth, of being without money, of fines, of tax collectors, of theft, of losing money or power, of not being eligible for a job or medical insurance, of being unable to repay a mortgage, of not getting a job or of losing it, the list is endless…

Whether it is a monarchy, a democracy, a socialist or any other form of government these fears persist. Whether we are atheists, Christians, Muslims, Hindus, Sikhs, Buddhists, Jews, Parsis, Bahais or say that we believe in another religion, all these fears are with us in the modern world. And, most of them are due to the mind-set we have developed because of blindly following what we have been dictated to follow by the society we live in.

In short, despite our preachers and political leaders or because of them, we have developed a society based mainly on fear which leads to all kinds of criminal and other negative thought and activity. All of us may not be criminals in the legal sense but in thought, word and deed we have committed crimes against others and against ourselves in the form of stress and mental torture to both ourselves and others. We have ill-will towards many, verbally or even physically abuse some and dwell in fears mentioned above ourselves. We live in fear which causes stress and leads to ill-health, the very thing we fear!

It is not possible nor, perhaps, desirable for society to totally eradicate fear at this stage of development for that could lead to chaos and destruction rather than peace and harmony of mind, body and spirt leading to a better overall environment for sentient beings. Total elimination of fear, if it were possible, should only be attempted in beings who are perfect or very nearly so – those who not only understand but have realized the essence of religion based on their spiritual development. That time may or may not come on earth but the reduction of fear to a great extent is possible through good education that promotes positive, logical thought and can lead us to an evolutionary stage not yet witnessed on our planet nor likely to happen without the near elimination of fear.

Notes & References

1. Mencken, H.L. (n.d.) 'Minority Reports Quotes'. *Goodreads*. Retrieved on 12 oct. 2020 from

https://www.goodreads.com/work/quotes/63090-minority-report-maryland-paperback-bookshelf

2. Macauley, T.B. (02 Feb. 1835). 'Minute by the Hon'ble T.B. Macauley.' Retrieved on 12 Oct. 2020 from

http://www.columbia.edu/itc/mealac/
pritchett/00generallinks/macaulay/
txt_minute_education_1835.html

3. Deepi. (2020) *You, Me and Little I*. Deep Eye Creations, Canada.

4. Gandhi, Mahatma. (n.d.) *Forbes Quotes on the Business of Life*. Retrieved on 12 Oct. 20202 from

https://www.forbes.com/quotes/6245/

5. Dante. (n.d.) 'Inferno (Dante): Eighth Circle (Fraud). Canto XXVIII, Bolgia 9.' *Wikipedia*. Retrieved on 16 Aug. 2020 from

https://en.wikipedia.org/wiki/Inferno_(Dante)

6. 'Charlie Hebdo attack: Three days of terror.' (15 Jan.2015.) *BBC News*. Retrieved on 16 Aug. 2020 from

https://www.bbc.com/news/world-europe-30708237

7. 'Jesus was a Buddhist Monk' (n.d.) *BBC Documentary*. Dailymotion. Retrieved on 18 Aug. 2020 from

https://www.dailymotion.com/video/x6ynf9o

8. Pascal, Blaise. (n.d.) 'Blaise Pascal: Finding God in Revealing Fundamental Truths of Life.' *League of Everyday Doxologists*. Retrieved on 13 Oct. 2020 from

https://www.doxologists.org/blaise-pascal/

9. Some of the ideas, even sentences in this book may seem repetitive but they are repeated so that they are clear to and remembered by most readers.

CHAPTER 5: THE SOLUTION

Something like the conversation below took place a few years ago in an academic institution. The conversation is not complete nor are the exact words given as what was said was not recorded but most of the **ideas are there.**[1] Here is the duologue:

Mike: How can you say there's no difference between religions?

Denise: I'm not denying the minor differences, I'm just saying there's no basic difference between them for they all talk about the beginning of the world, the deterioration of humankind from a perfect or near perfect state and they talk of the end of the world and that we need to love one another.

Mike: But what about things like reincarnation that the Hindus believe in and our belief in heaven?

Denise: Do you remember when Jesus says Before Abraham was, I am?

Mike: Yes, I do. What about it?

Denise: When does he say it?

Mike: When he says Abraham was happy to see his day coming and is asked how he could have met Abraham when he, himself was so young and not born at the time.

Denise: Right, so what do you think he means?

Mike: I'm not really sure, but I've heard it somewhere it means he is beyond time.

Denise: But no one asks him what he means which implies those in that time and culture understood it. To me, it seems very similar to the conversation Lord Krishna had with Arjuna in the

Bhagvad Gita.

Mike: And what was that?

Denise: When Krishna says he gave knowledge to the sun-god "in the beginning" and Arjuna asks him how that's possible as the sun-god is very senior to him, Krishna replies that they have both gone through many births and deaths and while he, Krishna remembers them all, Arjuna does not. This was written much, much before the Bible was.

Mike: You mean reincarnation is a part of Christianity? What about heaven then, and the second coming?

Denise: Heaven is a place with sidewalks of gold for some, for the Muslim males it's a place with beautiful virgins while for the is very Buddhist it's Nirvana. To me its symbolic and means a condition of blissful peace. As far as the second coming is concerned, the Christ appearing in the clouds or sky simply means that when this happens there will be no doubt in anyone's mind, it will be a moment of self-realization for all so we should not be misled by false prophets.

Mike: That's crazy.

Denise: Perhaps it is to you but remember Mike, Jesus understood Eastern philosophy and symbolism well. In fact, one of my friends feels the three wise men from the East who visited him symbolise that and the star that led them is probably a sign that they were great astrologers.

Mike: You and your friend are crazy. Next, you'll say the theory of Karma is part of Christianity as well.

Denise: I can't say for sure as I can't be certain of any of my beliefs but the Bible does say that we must reap what we sow which seems to indicate something like that. And yes, before you question me about Christ sitting on the right hand of God, I think it is completely symbolic and, like the Holy Trinity means becoming one with God.

Mike: You're so Hindu in your thoughts! And why couldn't Jesus say all that plainly?

Denise: The people he was talking to could not even understand the parables without his explaining them, how could they have understood deeper philosophy? For example, when the Bible talks of the sins of parents visiting their children it could mean the theory of genetics as we know it today. It's something like the ancient Indian yogis telling the people they should not sleep under the trees after dark as there were ghosts on them. They could not explain the concept of oxygen and carbon dioxide to the ordinary folk of the time so they instilled fear in them. (End of duologue)

The conversation continued for some time and turned into an argument but that is not important. The important point that is brought out is the fact that most religions of the world say that the universe was created, it will end and that people's character has deteriorated and we must live a life that takes us more and more towards love and peace. Whether it is the law of karma that motivates us into doing it or the commandments of God, the end result is the same. However, people like Mike above are not mentally prepared to listen to such logic for the simple reason that they have been trained to follow what they hear others say; whether it be their parent, preacher or politician, they find it more convenient to agree with them than to think on their own.

As most of us, especially at home, school and at religious places, have been conditioned to think like Mike - to look for differences rather than similarities in different religions, races and cultures - we are very likely to be exploited by some political and other leaders who follow the policy of divide and rule.

We need to reiterate that political and other leaders have used race, religion, money and other means to divide the people through one kind of fear or another and gained power in the past, are still using these methods and will keep on doing the same unless we, the people do something to force them out of it. There are at least two questions that we need to think about, if not answer directly in this context: What can be done so that people learn to think on their own in a positive manner which promotes love and peace? What needs to be done about the people who have already been conditioned into thinking in a narrow, negative or selfish way?

At this moment, we will not dwell further on or argue about whether or not it is because of leaders and preachers who influence parents and teachers who, in turn, sow the seeds of racial, religious and other kinds of superiority/inferiority into the innocent minds of children as the fact remains that most children, from an early age, get these and many other negative ideas ingrained into their psyches which is a recipe for discord in society and stress in the individual. It is also totally against the basic tenets of religious spirituality which implies true religion as the enlighteners of souls saw it and wanted to spread among the peoples of the world.

Before we discuss how to solve these problems, let's talk about a small country and its king who behaved very differently from the people in power in the rest of the world. We briefly mentioned this country earlier but now it is time to go into a little more detail. Like no individual human is perfect, no country can be perfect but we need to try and move sincerely towards the ideals of love, peace and inclusion that lead to perfection. This has surely been the endeavour, most times, of the king of the small but enchantingly beautiful Himalayan Kingdom of Bhutan – 'The Land of the Peaceful Dragon.'

Bhutan is a landlocked country with two large countries – India and China- on its borders. Even when 'the sun never set over the British Empire' and India lost its independence to the British, this small country remained free. As per its constitution, Bhutan has to have at least 60 % of its land under forest cover. It has always succeeded in its target. Capital punishment was abolished in 2004. There were problems with the Nepali speaking population of the country and large numbers had to go to Nepal as refugees but thereafter it has returned to its customary tradition of peace and tranquillity. This is a country which not only has immense natural beauty but also people with a pure mind. King

Jigme Singhye Wangchuk not only voluntarily gave up most of his administrative powers to make Bhutan move towards democracy but also gave the world the concept of Gross National Happiness in place of Gross National Product. We will try and answer why, despite not being evil, most of the leaders do not work for the people and the world as sincerely as King Wangchuk.

Why are most people, including those in power, not like the king of Bhutan or better? Why do people, whether they are monarchs, military dictators, democratically elected or simply appointed CEOs and others cling to power even if it means stepping over the happiness and rights of others, despite knowing fully well that neither they nor their progeny will live forever? Why do we all try and amass money? Why do we compete with others and become proud of our 'successes' and pull others down? As it is said in some religious texts, each one of us "lives in a body of clay but is arrogant" as if s/he will live forever. Why does this happen?

The answer to the questions posed in the two previous paragraphs is quite simple: our education has been faulty and we fail to realize the truth even when we see it all the time before us. Instead of improving our systems of education which were traditionally based on one religion and included its redundant laws and rituals, we have either remained stuck up with the same or have worsened it by removing religion and not providing anything in its place to fill the void. To worsen matters, we have included competition with others instead of setting time-bound targets for each student to make them better than they were the month or year before. Our education and all other systems we have developed due to it have just promoted unhealthy, sometimes dishonest competition among people, provinces and countries but failed to give us the realization of the Buddha despite seeing numerous sick, old and dead people…

An old story may be relevant here: A tourist, having heard of a wise hermit went to visit her. She lived alone in a small cave in the hills which was not too far from the city. The tourist, carrying her small backpack walked up the hill till she arrived at the cave. The hermit sat outside, basking in the sun.

"I have heard a lot about your wisdom," said the tourist.

"They say I am wise for they know not there are no wise...' was the enigmatic comment.

"Do you mind if we go in? I'd like to see how you live," the tourist showed her curiosity.

"Sure, we can talk more comfortably inside and have what little I can offer you," the hermit invited her as if to a luxurious living room.

The tourist was surprised to see the spartan lifestyle, there were just a couple of blankets, a small stove, few clothes and fewer utensils. There was hardly anything in the cave - even that which a minimalist today would consider 'essential stuff' was missing.

"You don't have much in here, how do you manage to live?"

"How do you manage to live? You can't carry much with you in your small backpack..."

"But this is enough for me, I'm just a tourist."

"So am I," was the reply which led to a more detailed conversation. They had a good discussion after which the tourist emptied most of what was in her backpack and, as soon as she returned home, donated most of what she had and learnt to live with the bare minimum. This is what true education needs to teach us, not only for the environment but for our own good and happiness. We look for the pleasures and luxuries of life which give us stress and cost us our happiness, freedom and fearlessness for the more comforts and luxuries we have, the more afraid and stressed we are of losing them. Education needs to make us aware of this fact and leave the choice to us.

So, how can we get more, if not all people, to behave like the hermit in the story? Where can we learn these truths and the right way of life that can lead to stress-free living? There is a true story from the life of the author's maternal grandfather (as told to him by his mother) which may take us towards the solution… Dharam Anant Singh, who despite facing great problems in life remained stress-free and died (almost penniless) in his nineties. He came from a rich, landlord family in the Punjab, India. Like many rich people of the time, his father wanted him to study in England so, to fulfil his father's dreams and his ambitions he set off for the country known for its excellent education and much more. It was some time in the early 1900s that the young Dharam, probably between eighteen and twenty years of age at the time, boarded the ship to England determined to get his engineering degree from that country.

While on the ship, he met an Englishman and both of them started talking to each other. During the course of the conversation, the Englishman told him a story. It was a thought-provoking story, a philosophical story but the young man had heard it before. His mother had told the exact same story when he had been much younger but he remembered it distinctly. He also remembered the name, 'Aflatoon' which his mother had mentioned. However, the Englishman referred to him as 'Plato.'

Were Plato and 'Aflatoon' the same or different men? Had the Greeks stolen an Indian idea or was it the other way around? The young Dharam wondered and thought about it during the rest of his journey. He was determined to find out the truth and to study the man or men more thoroughly. This delayed his engineering degree but he published his first book in England at the young age of 20 or 21, no mean achievement for an Indian at that time. He had many other achievements to his credit but there were a lot of struggles and testing times he had to go through which left him penniless towards the end of life but he remained a calm and composed man radiating a strange happiness till he passed away at a ripe, old age.

When he was young, the author's mother also told him stories of Nanak, Vivekananda, Socrates and others who talked of peace and goodwill. As he grew older, he was lucky to have his grandfather's huge personal library at his disposal and also great teachers one of who, Brother P.F. O'Keeffe kindled in him a love for reading. Brother O'Keeffe had a class library in which each student had to donate a book. He himself had donated some classics. Every week, in the library period, he would pick up a classic and talk about it creating an interest in the author and the book. Then, he would tell some of the children in the class to read some parts of the book which he had pre-selected for them to read. These served as teasers for the class and everyone wanted to find out more about the story. The teacher quietly placed a few more copies of the book so that everyone would get a chance to read the classic.

Brother O'Keeffe also conducted Moral Science lessons in which he discussed everything from sex to super-consciousness and his pupils had the freedom to talk of other religions and their experiences with them.

The facts above have been mentioned to show that if parents and grandparents tell children thought-provoking stories and their teachers guide them into reading books that encourage them to think positively and independently, they will learn to separate the grain from the chaff and not be easily duped by the politician, the preacher and even writers who have some political or other axe to grind by deliberately or otherwise misguiding the public. This solution, though, will need to be modified to deal with the challenges posed by the universal presence of computers, the internet and paucity of time which most parents complain of today.

The best, wherever possible, would be if parents could spend more time with their children, read out good books to them if they are not well-versed in the art of telling stories and then the job is taken over by the teacher at school but if parents cannot do the needful, the next best thing would be to light the little candles at school. For that, though, there would be the problem of suitable teachers and of moral education in the true sense of the term which implies education for love, peace and equality.

The present systems of education, in most parts of the

world, permit anyone and everyone who completes a degree in education/teaching to teach. This is useful in the sense that people who take up the teaching profession for various reasons get enough skills to teach a prescribed curriculum with some level of competence which enables their students to be eligible to get jobs; however, the enthusiasm, the zeal so essential for a teacher to kindle the fire of love for reading and for humanity, to instil in their pupils the courage and confidence to think independently, rationally, positively and passionately about the future of sentient beings is virtually impossible to learn by merely obtaining a degree for this passion comes naturally to a teacher who is sincere and feels for the students – s/he is not only similar to a true 'enlightener' of souls but can transform many of her/his students into beacons of light for others to follow. Such teachers are rare.

Anita Lawrence (AKA 'Lucy Miss') has been such a teacher since the time she started teaching at the young age of 14, in a school started by her mother, Mrs. C.R. Lawrence. Many of Anita's students worship her and, during the time this book was being written, a former student of hers who was just three or four years old when she was taught by her discovered her on social media. Her former classmate was already in touch with the teacher. Here is a part of the conversation between them as seen on Facebook.

Anita Lawrence: Time Flies, two students...and...got in touch with me, shared wonderful memories when as a young teenager, I taught these two wonderful children who are now doing extremely well in life. God bless you my dear children, keep rising keep growing!!Lots of love and blessings!

Student: Though I have come a long way and have seen many ups and downs till now, but never forgot the fact that ...the gains I have achieved throughout and the capacity to face challenges was provided through my foundation which was laid by you people. I often used to wonder, how it was possible that I have never forgotten my Lucy miss and my childhood friends even after four decades.... the answer that I get from myself is that the early imprints on a child's mind and psyche should be imprinted with deep love, bonding, personal concern, on spiritual level and with high standards. I feel proud that you have done all that.

Though it was a small set up in a small town, it was capable of inculcating deep values into the children like me. I have never forgotten those Moral science book chapters that were read with so much depth and reality. The high standard of extra-curricular activities in the form of annual functions, in which I was made to participate in every item, has built up confidence in me which is helping me till date. The lessons of correct pronunciation have also worked for me for my performing arts till date. I have never forgotten the sweet name "Lucy Miss" and have kept waiting to see her fondly throughout all these years. The group photo that you have shared and all other photos were like some holy scripture, which I have crammed madly throughout my childhood days and afterwards.

They say what you wish for, HE will fulfil! And they say the World is so small!... It happened and I found you and ... (name of her classmate) here on Facebook.

I danced with joy the day I saw your name in somebody's post and confirmed that It was you.... I had searched for... (classmate's name) many years back on fb...but in vain!

I still remember your hair style (seen in this photo) ... And I remember the names of my classmates this photo too.... Some are......and cry baby me (though I was a chirpy child but you know why I was crying here...hehe!

Thanks to God for providing a chance to know about you again!

Thanks for being there!

Thanks for being YOU my Lucy Miss!

I still have my nursery report card with your hand writing and have got it laminated many years back.

I am waiting for the day...when I shall meet you! Amen!

Another student, a classmate of the one above, writes on his experience: Dear Lucy Ma'am, we were blessed to have a teacher like you, I remember when I was lagging behind in Punjabi subject, you studied Punjabi then you taught me the same, till date whatever Punjabi I can read is because of you, this is one of a kind memory I'm sharing, there are plenty of them which I still cherish, I can write a small book on that, in a few words I just want to say you are an ocean of knowledge, it's up to a student how much they can learn from you ma'am,

Thanks once again respected ma'am, whatever I am today is the learning base which was made by your own very hands, keep teaching, preaching - our future generations need you very much so keep on enlightening

With all my gratitude, I will always be grateful.

(End of Facebook excerpt. Please note that the students' names have been removed as the author did not have the requisite permission to mention their names)

These are just two of the numerous compliments she has received from students of all ages who she has taught in the past over four and a half decades. These have been picked up as they are the most recent ones and also the oldest in the sense that they are from the first or second year of her teaching career. She has taught students who have been two years old to those who are in their thirties and has been loved by all of them regardless of their age, country and the subjects taught.

This great teacher and human being, when she started teaching, had no degree in education (or any other degree for that matter.) In fact, when after she got married and joined a reputed school in another city, she was given a lower salary than most other teachers in that school because the school/government rules did not permit a higher salary for her! The Principal who had appointed her loved her but she was unable to give her an appropriate salary as she did not have the requisite degree in education! The love of students, the Principal's appreciation, the teacher's passion and dedication were of no avail as the rules, the system was blind to these facts of emotion. The rules created by the system ostensibly followed the head, not the heart but ended up following neither for one invariably depends on the other. The right balance in life is necessary as a headless heart and a heartless head are both equally detrimental to not only the individual but to society as well.

Brother O'Keeffe had no degree in education, he was among the best and most loving among the teachers the author has ever come across. He used to teach Moral Science and English. Many of the teachers, the best and the most loving he remembers at the college and university level had neither a degree in education nor had completed their Ph.D. but they all loved their students, had mastered their subjects, were passionate about their teaching and were very good human beings who wanted to make a difference in the world.

What has been said in the previous paragraphs in no way detracts from the character or excellent work many of the highly qualified people like Noam Chomsky and the author's former teacher Dr. D.C. Saxena do but is to try and show that degrees are not prerequisites nor always essential for teachers to be passionate and successful in shaping their students' humane behaviour.

People with degrees in education or doctorate degrees are very likely to successfully train students to pass exams and equip them for jobs but they may or may not have the capacity or the inclination to guide students into being better human beings for they, themselves, have been trained to earn degrees and get employment and not to improve society or to become and make better people. Their role, too, is important for we need and will always need degrees and employment but their training should also include a detailed study of how to improve human behaviour and a basic study of how various religions and poetry can be used to improve their students' emotional character and thought processes so that greed, selfishness and other negative qualities can be discouraged and rational, positive thought encouraged for emotional development leading to peace and reduced stress.

No formal moral training of two, three or four years will modify the way most of the teachers who receive this training think and behave but it may change some and will make all of them aware of their duty and give them some sort of understanding that they will consciously or subconsciously imbibe and, at some stage, pass on to their students. This is not likely to have a great effect on them because the basic aim of these teachers will be to make the children learn to read and write and prepare them for jobs. It is for this reason, that we need to have other people who teach them the values of honesty, fearlessness, compassion, hard work and other human values which children need so much especially since the void created by the decline of religion and proliferation of the internet in most countries.

Unfortunately, most countries have not thought of how to fill the gaps created by the decline of religion and a lack of time leading to little or no guidance from parents. Besides, they have been unable to check the negative impact of the internet and other technologies like the cellular phone. These problems have worsened due to an ever-increasing number of divorce cases and live-in relationships that do not last very long and the consequent increase of single parent households with the parent getting no or very little time with the children, let alone enough time for moral guidance. So, what can be done about this?

Along with the regular, trained teachers who specialize in at least one subject, three hours per week of teaching by teachers who we could term 'born teachers' passionate about making the world a less selfish and more peaceful place should be made mandatory. Such teachers could be people running NGOs, famous personalities known for their work in world peace or even regular teachers who sincerely want to make a positive impact on the world through their students. It would be best if such people be physically present in their classes but, if that is not possible, technology could be used to provide online classes.

Something of this sort, in the form of Driglam Namzha,

is being attempted in the Land of the Peaceful Dragon (Bhutan) since the 1980s but needs to be updated and improved to counter the ever-increasing negativity which is now a part of social and other media.

The Driglam (order, discipline, culture and traditions) Namzha (system) prevalent in the schools of Bhutan is, no doubt, a good attempt but needs to change with the realities of the modern world of social media and the internet. It does not, still, fully take into consideration the fact that the Bhutanese are now aware of and influenced (both positively and negatively) by what happens in other parts of the world through the internet and travel. This needs to change and so most of the suggestions in the following paragraphs can also be used in Bhutan. Along with Bhutanese tradition and culture, for example, the positive qualities found in other traditions, cultures and religions need to be taught. Had this happened earlier, perhaps, the Nepalese from Southern Bhutan would still be there and would have enriched the country with their love and diversity.

Let us now move onto talk about the world, in general. The teachers who conduct these classes for making students more compassionate and thoughtful need not have degrees but should have a passion to teach, a fair and humane outlook on life and the will to create people with a better understanding of life, a will to improve themselves, to learn from wherever they can, an open mind, honesty and integrity and other related qualities besides having sufficient knowledge of various religious texts. It appears to be a tall order but many such people are available and will come forward once the requirement of a degree in education is removed.

People from diverse fields may be willing to work for schools a few hours every week and may work free or for a very low salary as they will have other full-time jobs and will be teaching the kids as they believe in what they say and love to teach it to others. There are many such people who work for NGOs and religious institutions so, if they are given the opportunity, they would be more than willing to serve schools on a part-time but regular basis. Another good idea could be to encourage and train old, retired people to teach these values to young children at school or in special camps organized for them and supervised by prominent people known for their honesty and integrity.

The culture and traditions these teachers teach may be of the area in which the institution is situated (provided they do not go against humanity as a whole or against any social or religious group) but the discipline and human values that are taught have to be universal. This can be more clearly explained through examples:

Traditionally, in some Asian countries, people wear white clothes at the time of death while the tradition of wearing black on this occasion is common in the west. There is no problem with such traditions that are part of two different cultures as they do not go against humanity in any way and no one is affected whether people wear black or white in a funeral procession. On the other hand, there was a tradition in India called *Sati* in which the widow was burnt alive; in America, slaves were ill-treated and even killed. Similarly, there have been many brutal traditions in most parts of the world and discrimination still persists in one form or another. Any such tradition that ill-treats or discriminates cannot form part of any modern curriculum or culture. Those countries that do not follow these guidelines will need to be coerced by other countries and the United Nations to do the needful.

The teachers who teach these values will have to be clear that traditions and cultures change with time and need to change for the progress of humanity. Just as Sati is no longer part of the Indian culture, slavery has been wiped out of the USA, all kinds of discrimination must also end the world over.

These teachers will need to be aware that a person can be made ashamed of almost anything. There was a time when women were made to feel ashamed of their pregnancy, menstruation was a dirty word, divorce was taboo and being gay was looked down upon. As a character in Aldous Huxley's 'Point Counterpoint' puts it:

"Absolute and natural rubbish!' said Rampion indignantly, 'shame isn't spontaneous, to begin with. It's artificial, it's acquired. You can make people ashamed of anything. Agonizingly ashamed of wearing brown boots with a black coat, or speaking with the wrong sort of accent, or having a drop at the end of their noses. Of absolutely anything, including the body and its functions. But that particular shame's just as artificial as any other. The Christians invented it, just as the tailors in Savile Row invented the shame of wearing brown boots with a black coat. There was precious little of it before Christian times. Look at the Greeks, the Etruscans." **(Huxley)**[2]

It was because of such problems created by religious preachers who took the laws as permanent or misinterpreted religion and that writers like Huxley had to speak against religion and the baby was thrown out with the bathwater, the philosophy of religion went out with the laws and rituals and the greatest reform of Christ that the laws (represented by Sabbath) are made for man and not man for the law was forgotten. This decline in the role of religion left society with a vacuum that could not be successfully be filled by science for it focused just on the 'how' ignoring the 'why' which religion in its philosophy had always tried to answer. Many of the frustrated youth and others who wanted to know the 'why' and not just the 'how' either took to drugs or other forms of 'relief' while some were misled by preachers, godmen and godwomen into superstition, if not violence.

Of course, what the character created by Huxley said in the quote above was a reaction and could lead to the other extreme so there has to be a balance. Being ashamed on the basis of race, caste, religion, some physical or mental deficiency and similar things is simply not right, religious or spiritual and should be socially unacceptable for a society. On the other hand, people have to be ashamed and of indiscipline, corruption, murder, rape and so on. Whenever we say people should not be afraid, it means courage of the true sort and righteous fearlessness by which is meant the ability and courage to work towards compassion, equality and love without an element of fear for other kinds of 'fearlessness' are based on fear e.g. 'fearlessness in competition is based on the fear of the 'opponent' being better at some skill and winning.

All teachers, even if they teach just science or social studies, must understand these concepts so that they desist from shaming their students or misguiding them in any way. This needs to be an essential part of their training and the teachers who teach the discipline, acceptable behaviour and human values must give them refresher courses every year to ensure that all teachers follow what they have been taught. If it is found they do not, they would need to go off teaching and be trained in these essentials by a suitable person. If the teacher repeats such behaviour three times, s/he would not be eligible to teach, just as paedophiles are not allowed to teach children today. It may seem difficult and even impractical but that is simply because it has yet not happened. Once the will to do it is created, it will not be long before it is 'made' practical.

Now, we need to consider how to make the students learn to question beliefs and find the answers that can make them better and more compassionate human beings. The answer, strangely, lies in religion though not in the religion of the preachers who concern themselves with the laws and rituals but with the preachers and school teachers of discipline and human values who are seekers of truth and try to truly understand the true enlighteners of souls. These people will need to study different religious scriptures to familiarize themselves with the laws, rituals and philosophies of various religions as given in the scriptures and then try to find the common and useful elements relevant for today's world which they would be required to teach the children and to encourage discussion on different religious beliefs by them.

When we discuss religion, we must be careful of a few

things. We need to approach it in a positive way to see how we can become better human beings, not with an eye of negative criticism that looks for faults like apparent discrepancies or how one religion is different from another. As in an example given in a previous chapter where the gods, humans and asuras approach Brahma for advice, religious books are not written for one person or a group that thinks in a similar manner. The scriptures have to cater to people of various intellects and in various stages of physical, mental and spiritual development. They attempt to serve all at their levels and we must get what is relevant to us e.g. a scripture might talk about the power and anger of God in an attempt to make a certain type of person fear God before s/he is fit enough for grace and love which may be the most important message of that scripture. Such a person e.g. a hardened criminal may have never understood the meaning of love and respect and has to learn to improve a little through the fear of God before s/he gets to the stage where the real message of love can get through.

Especially when dealing with children, it is important to be very careful when discussing things like forgiveness. It would be appropriate, here, to repeat an example that has been given earlier in a different context. When we talk of love and forgiveness, we must keep in mind the other side too. The Bible talks of the importance of forgiveness and Jesus goes to the extent of saying that we ought to forgive seventy times seven. It should be made very clear to the children that the Christ never said that we should forget. We need to clarify that when he talks of being as innocent as the dove, he also qualifies it with being as cunning/wise as the serpent. The children must be aware that we need to forgive but also protect ourselves by not forgetting how we have been wronged for, if we forget, we can be duped and taken advantage of again. They must be told the story of Joseph in the Old Testament to make the point clear to them. We need to ensure that children have an open mind, become loving and gentle but not be fooled by criminals and others who may want to harm them.

Sometimes we suffer from delusions of our own creation.

We 'help' others in their misdeeds or do something we should not do for others thinking of them as friends or family. There is an old story in which a dacoit loots and kills people to serve his family. Once he comes across a saintly person in the forest where he operates. This person asks the dacoit why he loots and kills and if he is not afraid of God. The dacoit answers he is not afraid of anyone and he works to look after and feed his family. The next question of the saintly person is if his family would be willing to share the punishment for his misdeeds to which he receives an answer in the affirmative. He tells the dacoit to bind him and go and to confirm with his wife and children.

"No," they all answer, "it is your duty to feed us and we are not concerned with how you do it so we will not undergo any punishment for you."

The former dacoit goes back, sets the man who had opened his eyes free and meditates for years on end, till at last he understands the love and compassion of God.

All the ideas given above and much more is explained beautifully in old religious texts and the scriptures. These ideas were important when they were written hundreds, sometimes thousands, of years ago but are still relevant today while other ideas which are based more on the culture or tradition of the time rather than on philosophy have become redundant e.g. when the idea of having up to four wives was given by the Prophet Muhammad, he had made a major reform as before then there had been no restriction, in many communities, on the number of wives a man could have. And, to make it more difficult (virtually impossible) to have four wives, he said that they all had to be treated equally.

Let's now discuss the kinds of fear and fearlessness a bit more as it is of paramount importance to be clear about it when we teach children. The kind of fearlessness that is appropriate has already been discussed but can briefly be stated again as negative fears like that of unemployment, the exploiter and loss of any sort. The positive fears would include fears like the fear of justice whether it be through the laws of Nature, God or wo(man). Such positive fears are part of schooling and of most religion and need not be discouraged unless they go against human values which, in any case, would make them negative fears.

We can now talk about how we can ensure that our systems of education are geared to make our students fearless or, at least, to make them unafraid of most kinds of situations and to accept others with dignity while be scared of harming others and having a negative attitude what we term 'positive fear.' Secondly, we need our education to teach us love and compassion for humans (if not for all sentient beings) and to eliminate hatred completely. Thirdly, education needs to teach children respect for all religions and to understand the difference between the laws and rituals of religion on the one hand and its philosophy on the other. All this can only be achieved if they learn to think in a positive and rational way.

In short, the education system needs to make students not only to think rationally and independently but also think in a positive manner. The focus should not be on negative competition but on trying to perform to the best of one's ability and to ensure that the students become better and more efficient i.e. better in the sense of more compassionate and less selfish and more efficient in their studies or profession. The person teaching them human values would see to it that they become better and more rational human beings while their regular teachers would try and ensure they learn the conventional subjects in a way that encourages them to think independently in a logical manner and to compete with themselves rather than others and so become more competent as students and professionals.

First of all, the curriculum, for appropriate age groups, should clarify to the students the meaning of true courage and distinguish between fear that is negative and fear that is positive. they should know that true courage is doing the right thing both physically and morally and desisting from or 'fearing' to do the 'wrong' thing which implies harming sentient beings with malice or any other negative feelings in the head or heart. They should also be aware of how negative fear can harm the individual and society. These ideas will have to be reiterated from time to time at different levels of education till it is clear to the students that complete fearlessness can only follow after society passes through the sieve of positive fear. Almost all religious scriptures can be studied and discussed (at least three should be used) to clarify this point by those who teach human values and discipline. Similarly, love and peace are essential parts of all the works written or dictated by the true enlighteners of souls. These very religious texts and scriptures can give students the way to rational thought and respect for all religions through open discussions based on their readings.

As they mature, the study of a number of scriptures and critical discussions based on them will make the participants aware of the distinction between the laws and rituals which are for a period of time and the philosophy which is true for a long time, if not for all time. At this stage, atheistic philosophy can also be introduced and writers like Bertrand Russell can be discussed. This will make the students understand how similar their goals are to theistic philosophy and why there is no cause for hatred or exclusion of those who think differently even to the extent of not believing in the Almighty. Similarly, the views of gay and differently abled will need to be understood and accepted without being judgmental. Discussions on such subjects will teach students how to think in a rational and logical manner and to reach conclusions after a thorough analysis of what is being discussed. It will be a good exercise in taking thought to its logical conclusion and also give students a chance for self-analysis so that they know what is relevant for them in the scriptures and religions that they are studying. This experience in logical thought will complement their regular studies and help them in job interviews.

Another important aspect that will need to be discussed at various levels of education is the use of technology in an environmental and mind friendly way. We have already started thinking on making technology environment friendly but because of financial interests of big companies and businesspersons being involved, it is an uphill task. Add to that the fact that most effects of technological development are felt only after decades, it seems virtually impossible (at present) that technology will ever be totally environment friendly but if there are discussions at the school and college levels on how to make it a reality, it is very likely that it will happen.

Something which is not being talked about much is making technology body and mind friendly. We have to understand that many kinds of technology are a cause of mental stress and/or lead to a lack of physical activity, how to tackle these problems is already a major issue and is likely to get bigger unless we start discussing it much more seriously than we do now and find solutions at the earliest.

Every development in technology has made our lives better but has also taken away a lot. With the invention of the wheel came a lot of comfort and we could travel long distances but it led to physical inactivity. Similarly, the invention of the computer has enabled us to progress in numerous fields but an over-dependence on it may eventually be a cause of mental inactivity leading to a lack of competence in almost everything from maths to rational thought unless children are made aware of these problems at the middle and high school levels.

How to get out of the systems like that of taking everything on credit and leading a stressful life will also need to be thought about and the best time for this is student life, beginning at the high or even middle school level. Here, we may mention that whenever we say that something has to be discussed or thought about, the teacher must ensure that students' discussions do not deteriorate into argumentative debates. The discussions need to focus on new ideas to solve problems, not taking firm decisions based on personal beliefs and then trying to defend those decisions in a debate.

Once these aims of education are achieved and people do

not have negative fears and stop craving material luxuries, the godmen and women will 'vanish' on their own, the preachers and teachers will support if not become true enlighteners of individual souls and the world will be a much better place to live in. But now, the question is how can that be made possible? How can such systems of education be put in place in different parts of the world? For that, we - the people – first need to understand and then convince those in power that love, peace, honesty, sustained rational thought and positivity will benefit everyone without exception and it is not a utopian dream but a distinct possibility towards which we need to work and, if we do not work towards this vision and make it a practical reality, we will end up having the third world war and, as someone rightly said, it is most likely that the fourth will be "fought with sticks and stones" after the destruction caused by the third. This needs to be stressed by thinkers, writers and the media so that people and politicians are convinced of these facts.

Even if the second world war is the last great war, the result of hatred, negativity and terrorism will eventually have very similar disastrous consequences to those of a third world war. Hopefully, after the death and destruction caused by hatred or the next Great War, people will understand and there will be no war after that – even with sticks and stones. If any survive, they will have learnt their lesson and people will develop a system of education which will be something like what we are discussing here.

Our Prime Ministers and Presidents need to understand that it is better to realize the possibility of destruction and take remedial measures right away rather than wait for it to actually happen and hope some of us survive. The money presently being spent on weapons needs to go into the right kind of education and the elimination of poverty and disease. We, the people have to write, speak and do whatever else we can to convince the people in power that all this will be good for them and their families too.

The changes suggested above would make a difference only

after a few decades, can anything be done to improve the present scenario where most of us don't think, at least not positively? Of course, if even some people are sincere about making the world a better and more peaceful place. This idea was floated by the writer in his book, 'You, Me and Little I.' Let us quote straight from this book to get a clearer picture. Here is the excerpt:

"Education is a long process; do you think anything can be done to end terror and war in the next ten years?" Karen asked Dante.

"I will try and give a very practical solution and if we all try and implement it wherever we live, I think it'll surely have an impact."

"That's interesting, la. If we can actually do something, it'll be great, la." It was the quiet Thupten who spoke rather unexpectedly.

"Thank you, Thupten. What I propose is simple. We need to organize peace camps where people of different religions can come together and pray or meditate for the end to terror and for world peace."

"How d'you think that'll help?" Randall was sceptical.

"It will bring together people from different faiths and build bonds difficult to break by unethical leaders. This will stop terrorist activities and eventually end war."

"Yes Gupta ji, we could try out these prayer and meditation sessions in religious places of different faiths," Veer was excited, "our temple will love having people from other faiths coming in to pray for peace."

"So will our church," said Randall calmly.

"I'm not sure if it will be possible where I live, la. Not many people from other religions are there la," Thupten sounded a bit disappointed.

"All-faith meetings could be held in any hall if religious places are not available or, if you can't organize these meetings, you could just support those of us who are holding them," said Dante.

"What kind of support, la?"

"Support could come through meeting and writing to politicians and religious leaders to help the movement, advertising or writing about our mission in newspapers and so on...," Dante clarified.

. . .

"Once this happens, we can influence some religious leaders and clergy to influence the leaders of terrorist groups to attend these camps which can be organized once every week or fortnight," said Ghazala.

"We could even involve some politicians at some point," suggested Randall.

"They'll just mess up everything," countered Jyoti, "and it'll all end up with them fighting one another to get prominence."

"Once we influence the religious leaders and the movement catches on, the politicians themselves will be after us to be part of the program," said Veer.

"You're right Veer," said Dante, "but in some places people may need political support earlier, at other places even government permission may be required. Let the locals decide how they can help the mission become a massive movement according to the conditions where they live."

"Yes," said Thupten, "and we may even have to change the way we work according to place as well la, depending on the conditions."

"Very true," said Jyoti, "different ideas will be needed to tackle local problems, it's just the aim and the broad idea that will remain the same."

(Deepi)[3]

If we take the suggestions given in the dialogue above with

a positive attitude and a willing spirit that wants a better world, we - the people or even a single person, can do a lot for world peace at different levels and in various ways. It may seem far-fetched at the moment but there is nothing in it that is difficult to implement. Dr. Kiran Bedi, the first Indian woman police officer arranged meditation classes for hardened criminals which had a wonderful effect on them and changed them for the better. She won the prestigious Magsaysay Award for her efforts and became a household name in South Asia and beyond.

War, greed, rape, terrorism, theft, murder, hunting as a sport and similar acts are proof enough that we, homo sapiens, have become the craziest of animals over time which is why the Christ told us to be like little children implying the time before the child learns the 'ways of the world,' which means being like people in the beginning of the world, to be mentally and spiritually 'born again.' The time of innocence when we act without malice, we may say before Adam and Eve tasted the forbidden fruit which, in Indian philosophy. would be *satyug*, the era of truth when the world began. And to be in this state of innocence, we need to meditate, to be alone so that God, Mother Nature (the Universal Power) or our conscience can talk to us. It is for this reason that education, in the true sense, should also include meditation.

Meditation groups of children and adults for self-improvement and world peace in schools and elsewhere have become as necessary as they were found to be by Dr. Bedi in Tihar Jail of Delhi for we have lost our innocence and, consequently, the ability to communicate with the Universal Spirit. We may not be hardened criminals but our hearts have surely turned to stone which is why we lack kindness and compassion even at a young age.

Despite all efforts, despite giving the best of education (not mere good schooling for jobs}, there will remain some people who will insist on evil for adventure. Others may have or develop a perverted mind due to various factors including the inability to access good education or having faced some kind of abuse. Some such people may become leaders and be in a position to influence others till the time arrives when people are more highly educated in the true sense of the word. Going by our present levels of scientific, medical, mental and spiritual developments we cannot hope to tackle them in the near future simply with education, counselling and other measures suggested above. It may be necessary to jail them till the time individuals, society and science can deal with them in a better way.

So, what could be the best way to ensure that such people cannot harm society till they change? Perhaps more drastic action will be required for them for if a Hitler has once been created, s/he will need to be jailed or killed, there would be no other way except, perhaps, operating on his or her brain! But, it must be remembered that whatever action is taken needs to be taken in compassion, not malice. There is an incident from Gandhi's life in South Africa where he had to hit a student as there was no other way left for him, he hit him but cried as he hit him which reformed the student, not fully but to a great extent...

These strong measures will not be required (or will rarely be needed) after a few decades if we plan our systems of education well, keeping the facts and ideas discussed in this book in mind. The support of NGOs, writers and philosophers, philanthropists and world organizations like the United Nations could go a long way in forming and implementing such systems of education and reform.

In a bid to eliminate crime till the time better systems of education are implemented and can have a major effect, world identity cards would be a good idea. India's successful experiment with the Unique Identity (UID) Aadhar Number and card for each citizen has proved that it is possible to provide identity cards to large numbers of people. If what India has done for its huge population can be emulated by the United Nations at the world level, a data base can be created where each individual's details can be stored at the world level to which the government of each country can be given access. It would eliminate the need for passports as the criminal activities and behavior of each person could be part of this central database.

If such a research was to be undertaken, it would surely show that the money being spent on war and the preparations of war, if used sensibly, could end poverty and reduce sickness we see all around us. Since our leaders come from within us, they will also move towards perfection with the right education systems in place. We need to eliminate our fears through the right education which will eventually lead to a society free of war, crime, poverty and most disease. Meditation camps for adults and children not going to school, of course, would help in the interim.

Hope for such a society exists and it has been tried by advanced souls as shown by the experiment at Auroville. The **conditions in the commune**, according to some people, have **deteriorated**[4] with time but it may be a passing phase and it is very likely to show the world a new way as, if things can be managed well on a small scale for some time, they can also be handled on a large scale for an indefinite period of time, with better planning and execution which needs to keep pace with the developments both negative and positive.

Before we end with excerpts from a short poem by Tagore, it would be appropriate to mention another powerful quote from St. Theresa (formerly Mother Theresa): "May today there be peace within. May you trust God that you are exactly where you are meant to be. May you not forget the infinite possibilities that are born of faith. May you use those gifts that you have received, and pass on the love that has been given to you. May you be content knowing you are a child of God. Let this presence settle into your bones, and allow your soul the freedom to sing, dance, praise and love. It is there for each and every one of us." **(St. Theresa)**[5]

If what St. Theresa says happens in most of us, we could move towards positive and deep thought. This would make the following words of Tagore come true not just for one country but for the whole of our earth which would then be a place

"Where the mind is without fear…
Where the world has not been broken up into fragments by narrow domestic walls;
Where words come out from the depth of truth…
Where the mind is led forward by thee into ever-widening thought and action…"
(Rabindranath Tagore)[6]

May the Almighty give us wisdom and the capacity to work in the right direction, Amen!

Notes and References

1. Words and expressions used in the conversation are not the same as used by the speakers but the thoughts are. The participants' names have been changed and their number reduced to two from the original four to bring out the main ideas more clearly.

2. Huxley, Aldous. *Point Counter Point.* (n.d.). 'Aldous Huxley Quotable Quotes'. (n.d.) *Goodreads*. Retrieved on 13 Oct. 2020 from

https://www.goodreads.com/quotes/9826724-the-fact-of-shame-is-significant-we-feel-spontaneously-ashamed

3. Deepi. *You, Me and Little I.* Deep Inder (2020)

4. Crowell, Maddy. (24 June 2015.) 'Trouble in Utopia.' *Roads and Kingdoms.* Retrieved on 15 Oct. 2020 from

http://www.slate.com/articles/news_and_politics/roads/2015/07/auroville_india_s_famed_utopian_community_struggles_with_crime_and_corruption.html

N.B. The author visited the Commune in 1982 when it was a unique place with an air of positivity. No police or army was allowed in as per the rules. People from different parts the world and different walks of life lived there. They were very friendly and seemed to enjoy themselves. However, at the time, problems had started cropping up as he was told that, "till recently," it had been free but they had started taking a fee of Rs. 500 for the first month as some "locals had indulged in sexual harassment" and there were also "a few people who thought it was a good place to do drugs."

For those interested, the official information on Auroville can is available at:

https://www.auroville.org/contents/135

5. Dillon, Maureen. (n.d.) '14 Of the Most Powerful Peace Quotes From St. Teresa Of Avila.' *The Mystical Humanity of Christ Publishing.* Retrieved on 12 Aug. 2020 from

https://www.coraevans.com/blog/article/14-Of-The-Most-Powerful-Peace-Quotes-From-St-Teresa-Of-Avila

6. Tagore, Rabindranath. (n.d.) 'Gitanjali 35.' *Poetry Foundation.* Retrieved on 15 Oct. 2020 from

https://www.poetryfoundation.org/poems/45668/gitanjali-35

———

[TT1]

ACKNOWLEDGEMENT

First of all, I would like to thank Anita (my wife), Yasmin and Rubina (my daughters) and TJ (my son-in-law). All of them are most dear to me and I thank them for their constant and passionate support. My granddaughters, Alysha, Myra and Aria are equally dear and I thank them for always keeping me in good cheer. Next, i thank all my dear friends, relatives and teachers who have made me what I am today. Last, and perhaps the most, I thank Almighgty God for the inspiration, family, relatives, friends, critics, teachers and good health that made this work possible.

ABOUT THE AUTHOR

Deepi

Many of Deepi's articles and some short stories have been published in various newspapers and journals. He writes on a wide range of subjects for different age groups.

Deepi's first article, 'The Necessity of Irreligion' was published in the late 1970s or early 1980s and his first book, 'The invisible Path' (published by Authorhouse, USA), appeared in 2008. Peter Whitbread (Emmy Award, Writing) had really loved reading the book in its original form. This book was re-published as 'You, Me and Little I' after it was rewritten with a completely new ending. 'The True Enlighteners, Preachers and Politicians' is his first nonfiction work though he has written three other books before this one.

Deepi has visited many countries including England, Australia, the USA, Mexico and some EU countries. He has taught English

(ESL, Literature) in Canada, the Middle East, Bhutan and India. He is presently a full-time writer based in Regina, Canada.

BOOKS BY THIS AUTHOR

The True Enlighteners, Preachers & Politicians

Despite so many prophets and preachers, we are not happy and have made the world a place full of violence and crime. Is it possible to lead a less stressful life in a happier world? The author believes it is, and tells us how!

Adventures With Ajooba, The Magic Carpet

This book by Deepi is meant for children, 8-12 years of age. It comprises some moral stories incorporated in one magical story.

Planet Teen

Deepi writes of a planet ruled by teenagers that can teach us how to solve many of the problems of our own planet!

Be a part of their adventures as some teenagers from earth visit the strange planet on an invite from the Chief Teens!

You, Me And Little I

This is the author's first book, 'The Invisible Path' (published in 2008 by Authorhouse, USA) that has been rewritten with a completely new ending. The book tells of how a young man in India moves from a life of crime to that of a spiritually awakened person who works to make the world a better place.